The 24-Hour Fantasy with ChatGPT

Andrew Parry

Published by Andrew Parry, 2025.

THE 24-HOUR FANTASY WITH CHATGPT

First edition. April 19, 2025.

ISBN: 979-8230275329

Written by Andrew Parry.

Table of Contents

So You Want to Write a Fantasy Story Today 1

How ChatGPT Becomes Your Magical Writing Companion 3

Finding the Spark: Generating Your Fantasy Idea 5

What If...?: Prompting Your Way Into a New World 7

Starting with the End: Writing Backwards with Purpose 9

The Hero Is Everything: Designing Your Central Character 11

Creating Antagonists worth Battling 13

The Hero's Journey in Fantasy: A Template with a Twist 15

From Nothing to Kingdom: Building a Fantasy World in Minutes 17

Naming Your World, Its People, and Its Wonders 19

Maps in the Mind: Visualizing Fantasy Geography with Prompts 21

Let's Talk Magic: Creating Your Own Rules of Power 23

Magical Creatures: Breathing Life into Beasts and Beings 25

Gods, Spirits, and Mythologies: Inventing Fantasy Lore 27

ChatGPT as Your World-Building Co-Architect 29

Structuring the Story Before You Write 31

Three Acts and a Portal: Plotting Your Fantasy Adventure 33

The Prophecy Hook: Creating Urgency from Page One 35

The Chosen One and Other Classic Tropes You Can Use or Twist 37

Why Fantasy Needs Stakes: Creating Meaningful Conflict 39

Side Characters Who Steal the Show 41

The Mentor, the Trickster, and the Rival 43

Writing a Strong Opening Scene with AI's Help 45

Dialogue That Feels Real in Unreal Worlds 47

Describing Magic without Confusing the Reader 49

Giving Your Hero an Arc That Feels Earned 51

How to Build a Fantasy Culture in a Few Prompts 53

Politics and Power Struggles in Fantasy Realms 56
Rebellion, and Quest: Choosing Your Fantasy Plot Core 59
Love in the Realm of Dragons: Writing Romance in Fantasy 61
Integrating Mystery and Intrigue into Your Plot 63
Pacing the Adventure So It Never Drags 65
Emotional Highs and Lows: Writing Powerful Moments 67
When to Show, When to Tell in a Fantasy Setting 69
Using ChatGPT to Write Fast but Stay Creative 71
Creating an Ending That Feels Like Destiny 74
Editing in the Moment: Refining Paragraphs as You Go 76
Making the Magic Matter: Thematic Resonance in Fantasy 79
Generating Perspectives 82
What a Scene Looks Like in a Fantasy Screenplay 84
Turning a Story Idea into a Series with AI 87
How to Prompt for a Chapter That Writes Itself 89
Using Flashbacks, Dreams, and Visions to Deepen the Story 91
Creating Fantasy Titles That Grab Attention 94
Pulling the Reader Through with Cliffhangers and Curiosity 97
How to Write a Twist That Feels Like Fate 99
Using Your Own Voice While Working with AI 101
The Value of Archetypes in Fantasy Storytelling 103
Writing Across Cultures without Falling Into Stereotypes 106
How to Make Your Fantasy Feel Ancient and New 109
Finishing the Draft by Midnight: Pacing Your Writing Day 111
Using ChatGPT to Polish Prose and Fix Awkward Phrases 114
Testing the Logic of Your Magic System with AI 117
Checking for Plot Holes and Weak Character Arcs 120
Creating a Fantasy Story That Feels Real 123

Adding the Unexpected: Surprise Events and Sudden Turns 126
Formatting and Saving Your Story for Publishing 129
Cover Design and Blurb Writing with AI's Help 132
Sharing, Selling, or Just Savouring Your Finished Fantasy 135
Examples of Good Prompts for Fantasy Story Design and Structure 137
Examples of Good Prompts for Designing Compelling Characters 140
Examples of Good Prompts for World Building 143
Examples of Good Prompts for Ideas about Fantasy Stories 146
Your One-Day Fantasy Writing Game Plan – From Start to Publish 149
Doing It Again Tomorrow: Becoming a Fantasy Story Machine 153

So You Want to Write a Fantasy Story Today

You woke up today with a spark. Maybe it was a dream, a memory of a book you loved, or just that itch to finally write something fantastical. You want to write a fantasy story—dragons, magic, epic journeys, royal betrayals, enchanted forests, ancient runes, or talking swords. But here's the twist: you want to write it *today*. One day. Start to finish. And with ChatGPT by your side, that's not just possible—it's totally doable.

Writing a complete fantasy story in one day might sound like summoning a lightning bolt from a clear blue sky, but it's actually more like channeling a steady stream of energy. The trick is not perfection, it's momentum. You're not aiming for a polished masterpiece right out of the gate—you're chasing the raw, wild thrill of creating something magical from nothing. And that's where ChatGPT comes in—not to take over your creativity, but to fuel it. To be the voice in the void that helps shape the fog into form, one idea at a time.

Now, let's talk about fantasy. This genre isn't just swords and spells. It's about belief, possibility, myth, and transformation. Fantasy stories can be high and heroic, gritty and grim, whimsical, dark, or even modern and urban. The beauty is that *anything* goes, as long as the world makes sense on its own terms. That's part of what makes fantasy so freeing and fun to write. You get to break the rules—as long as you make new ones to follow.

But starting can feel like staring at a vast, unmapped land. Where do you begin? With a prompt. A question. A single sentence that lights the fire. ChatGPT is an idea machine, and you can start with the simplest prompt like, "Give me an idea for a fantasy story involving a cursed heirloom," or "What if magic was powered by memory?" And boom—you're off. One idea leads to another, then you ask for characters, a setting, and a basic outline. The beauty of this process is you're never stuck staring at a blank page alone. You always have someone—well, something—to bounce ideas off of.

You might be wondering how long your story should be. That depends on your energy and your goals. Are you writing a short story? A novella? The opening episode of a fantasy TV series? The process is the same. You brainstorm, outline, and write in fast, focused bursts. ChatGPT can help fill in gaps, expand scenes, and even throw in dialogue that sounds like it came from a seasoned bard. It's your imagination in overdrive, with AI providing the engine oil.

One important key is deciding early on how you want to work with ChatGPT. Some writers prefer to ask for a rough scene outline and then write the full paragraphs themselves, asking the AI only for ideas or feedback. Others go the other way and say, "Write me 500 words of this battle scene," and then they tweak or revise it afterwards. Neither way is wrong. What matters is that you stay in the zone and keep the story moving forward. Don't let your inner editor interrupt the flow. You're here to *create*, not critique.

Fantasy, more than any other genre, rewards the bold. Want to start in the middle of a war between talking wolves and fire priests? Do it. Want your hero to wake up with wings and no memory of how they got them? Great. The more committed you are to the vision—even a vision that starts with a random AI-generated idea—the more readers will be swept up in it. The first draft is not about logic, it's about heart. Magic. Movement.

And here's something fun: you can ask ChatGPT to surprise you. Literally say, "Give me a twist I didn't see coming," or "Make something unexpected happen in this chapter." It'll keep the adventure fresh and unpredictable, even for you. The story becomes a co-creation—half your vision, half your machine-sidekick's chaotic brilliance.

It's also important to remember that you don't have to go it alone, even when you're working solo. You can use prompts like "Write a conversation between a cynical mage and a talking cat about their failed heist," or "Describe an ancient ruined city swallowed by the forest, haunted by sentient vines." These sorts of prompts keep your mind inspired and your writing rich in detail, tone, and voice.

The pacing of your day matters too. Give yourself a couple of hours to brainstorm and outline. Then block out time for writing in chunks. Maybe 500 words an hour. If you're doing 6,000 to 8,000 words for a short fantasy novella, that's very doable in a day if you stick to it. Use ChatGPT to accelerate the slower parts—describe a location, write background lore, fill in conversations or flavor text. You can go deep fast.

So if you're ready to dive in, remember this isn't about writing the next Tolkien-level epic in a single day. It's about getting something *done*, something fun, something that feels alive. And once it's done? You've got the bones of a world, the spark of a hero, the path of a journey. You can polish it later. Maybe even turn it into a series. But today, you're doing the wild, brilliant thing of creating a fantasy story from scratch—and ChatGPT is your spell-book, your map, your squire, and your sword.

How ChatGPT Becomes Your Magical Writing Companion

Let's be honest. Writing a fantasy story in a single day sounds like something that requires either caffeine-fueled wizardry or a deal with a mischievous fairy. But here's the real secret weapon: ChatGPT. Not a replacement for your imagination, but a companion. A kind of enchanted quill that never tires, never complains, and always has another idea waiting just a prompt away. Once you understand how to work with this tool, it stops being just a chatbot and becomes something much closer to a magical writing partner—always ready, always brimming with possibilities.

Think of ChatGPT like the apprentice who can conjure a hundred versions of a scene or invent ten new types of magical creatures in under a minute. It doesn't get bogged down in fear or doubt. It doesn't stare at the blinking cursor, wondering if that sentence is good enough. It just *creates*. And when you're on a mission to write an entire fantasy story in a single day, that is the energy you want on your team.

To get started, you don't need to ask anything complicated. You can begin with a prompt as simple as, "Give me five ideas for a fantasy story." You'll be met with possibilities: an elf who trades memories for magic, a city built on the back of a giant turtle, a cursed crown that brings its wearer visions of the past. You take the one that grabs you—and that's your starting spark. Or maybe you combine two. Or ask for a twist. It's instant idea generation, and it removes the paralysis of "I don't know what to write."

Once you have an idea, you can ask ChatGPT to help you flesh it out. Want a protagonist who's both powerful and flawed? Ask it to describe a character who was born into royalty but rejects the throne in search of a magical truth. Want to create a villain with depth? Ask it to generate a character profile for a once-noble warrior corrupted by forbidden knowledge. You can even give it vibes to work from: "Make them sound like a tragic Shakespearean figure," or "Give them a sense of looming dread like a horror villain in a fantasy setting."

But what really makes ChatGPT magical is its versatility. It's your brainstorming partner, your scene sketcher, your dialogue drafter, and your world-building assistant—all in one. You can ask it to describe a setting in vivid, cinematic language, then immediately follow up with "Now rewrite that with more tension," or "Make it sound more ancient and mystical." It adapts to your style, your preferences, your pace.

It can also help you keep the story moving when your energy dips. That's one of the biggest roadblocks in same-day story writing: fatigue or writer's block creeping in halfway through Act Two. With ChatGPT, you can literally type, "I'm stuck. What should happen next?" and it'll throw five different directions at you—maybe the hero's mentor reveals a secret, or the artifact breaks, or the antagonist wins a small but critical victory. You get to pick what resonates and run with it.

Even better, ChatGPT remembers the tone and shape of what you're building as long as you keep feeding it context. So if your story's voice is poetic and grand, you can keep telling it, "Keep the dialogue epic and formal," and it'll adjust. Or if your fantasy is quirky and comedic, you can say, "Make the character sound sarcastic and modern," and it'll lean that way. The tool becomes an extension of your creative tone, your mood, your world.

You'll also find that ChatGPT makes the mundane parts of writing faster. Writing exposition about a centuries-old war that shaped your fantasy kingdom? Ask for a short mythic retelling. Need to explain the rules of your magical system but don't want it to drag? Ask for an in-world document like a spell-book excerpt or a wizard's lecture transcript. It gives you content in a variety of formats that keep things interesting for you and your reader.

And because fantasy thrives on immersion, description matters. That's another place where ChatGPT shines. You can write a rough paragraph and then say, "Rewrite this to sound more lush and atmospheric," or "Make this castle feel more eerie and haunted." It's like having a revision partner on standby 24/7, one who's never annoyed by your requests.

You can even test ideas quickly. Not sure whether your villain's motivation makes sense? Ask ChatGPT to analyze it like a story coach. Not sure if your opening scene hooks the reader? Ask it to simulate feedback from a reader's perspective. It can provide a second opinion instantly, and while it's not infallible, it's immensely helpful when you're writing on a deadline.

The other beautiful thing about this companion is that it doesn't judge. You can ask the weirdest, wildest questions—"What would a tavern menu look like in a world where everyone is part insect?" or "Describe a desert storm that rains hallucinations"—and it won't blink. It will just answer. That alone removes the self-censorship that kills creativity. It gives you permission to be bold.

Most importantly, ChatGPT keeps your momentum going. If you find yourself hesitating, stuck in a scene or searching for the next line of dialogue, just type something. Anything. "What would the villain say right now?" or "Give me five ways the protagonist could escape this trap." That's all it takes to get rolling again.

You don't have to use every word it writes. Often you'll find yourself tweaking, combining, rewriting. That's part of the magic—it becomes a conversation. Not just with the AI, but with the story itself. And the more you work this way, the faster your instincts grow. You'll get better at asking the right questions. Sharper at recognizing good ideas when they appear. Bolder with your own imagination, because you know you've got backup.

Writing fantasy in one day isn't about speed for speed's sake. It's about opening a floodgate. ChatGPT gives you the key. You still decide where the river flows, but you're no longer stuck trying to dig it out with your bare hands. You've got a magical spade, enchanted with infinite prompts, poetic phrases, twisty plots, and cinematic detail.

So yes—you can write a fantasy story in one day. And with ChatGPT as your magical writing companion, you're never alone in the process. Let's keep going. The realm awaits.

Finding the Spark: Generating Your Fantasy Idea

Before the dragons take flight or the cursed swords sing their ancient songs, before the kingdoms rise or fall, before you write even a single sentence of your fantasy tale, you need one thing: the spark. That little glimmer of an idea that makes you sit up straighter, that makes your fingers twitch, that whispers, *yes, this could be something.* Every fantasy story starts with a seed—and the good news is, with ChatGPT in your corner, planting that seed doesn't have to be hard or slow.

The pressure to come up with the perfect idea can be the first hurdle. People often think fantasy stories have to be big. Like world-shaking big. And sure, some are. But the core idea doesn't have to be massive to be magical. It just has to be compelling. And ChatGPT is built to generate compelling ideas quickly. All you need is a little curiosity and a willingness to explore.

You can start super simple. Just type: *Give me five fantasy story ideas.* And like a bard rifling through a dusty old scroll, it'll hand you concepts ranging from epic to intimate. You might get something about a forgotten god trapped in a child's mirror, or a floating city that's powered by dreams, or a witch who loses her magic every time she tells a lie. These might be rough, but they're yours to shape, twist, or combine into something unique.

You can also zero in on the kind of fantasy story you want to tell. Maybe you're feeling like writing a tragic romance between a human and a fae. Maybe you're in the mood for a grimdark revenge tale set in a crumbling empire. Maybe you want something cozy and whimsical with talking animals and sentient tea kettles. ChatGPT responds beautifully to genre-blending and tone-specific prompts. Try something like: *Give me a whimsical fantasy idea with a hint of mystery*, or *Suggest a fantasy story idea that starts in a jail cell beneath a haunted mountain.* The more specific your ask, the more tailored the response becomes.

Sometimes the best sparks don't come from fully formed plots—they come from fragments. A single image. A feeling. A line of dialogue. Ask ChatGPT: *Give me an opening line for a fantasy story*, or *Describe a magical object with a tragic history.* You'll find that these pieces often grow into something larger. A cursed amulet that causes visions. A prophecy written in disappearing ink. A storm that only strikes the same village once every hundred years. These are the raw ingredients. Your job is to pick the ones that taste right.

One powerful way to generate ideas is to start with a twist. Fantasy readers love a good "what if." What if the chosen one didn't want to be chosen? What if magic could only be cast by forgetting something important? What if the dragon everyone feared turned out to be a terrified child wearing armor made of illusion? Prompts like *Give me fantasy story ideas with unexpected twists* can spark stories that feel both familiar and fresh. It's the twist that often turns a basic concept into something that sticks with a reader.

Another great place to find your spark is by working backward from emotion. Ask yourself: what do you want this story to feel like? Nostalgic? Terrifying? Bittersweet? Ask ChatGPT to *give you a fantasy story idea that ends in heartbreak*, or *that feels like a dream you want to return to.* Emotion-led storytelling has power, and the AI can help you find a concept that's not just clever but resonant.

If you're stuck, you can also take inspiration from your favorite stories and then flip the script. What's your favorite fantasy novel, game, movie, or myth? Now ask ChatGPT: *Give me a story idea inspired by [insert title here] but with a new angle.* You might end up with a reimagined tale that still feels completely original. Change the roles. Set it in a different kind of world. Blend in a new genre. Add a time loop, a talking animal, a haunted machine. Fantasy loves reinvention.

You can also experiment with formats. Maybe you want to write something that feels like an old fairy tale, or like a letter from one character to another, or a journal found in the ruins of a forgotten civilization. Ask ChatGPT: *Give me a fantasy story idea told through journal entries*, or *a plot that could be written as an epic poem*. Sometimes changing the format gives birth to an entirely new kind of idea.

And if you're feeling brave, try a randomizer approach. Ask ChatGPT to mix unrelated elements: *Give me a fantasy story idea that includes a skeleton key, a snowfall that never stops, and a character who speaks only in riddles.* You might not know where it's going, but the collision of ideas can unlock a story that's far more original than anything you would've plotted traditionally.

There's no one way to find the spark. That's the joy of it. Fantasy is about breaking rules, creating new ones, and giving yourself permission to explore. And with ChatGPT, you're never stuck for long. Just when you think you've run out of ideas, you can throw another prompt into the cauldron and see what bubbles up.

The important thing is not to judge the idea too early. Let it breathe. Let it unfold. You can always revise, always reshape, always sharpen the vision later. For now, your only job is to light the fire.

Once you've got that spark, it's time to let it burn. The story will grow quickly if you feed it with questions, scenes, and characters. And just like that, your one-day fantasy writing journey begins—not with a grand outline or a massive plan, but with a single spark that becomes a flame.

Now that you've got your idea—or at least your starting glimmer—let's look at how to give it structure, purpose, and a direction that will carry you all the way to the final page.

What If...?: Prompting Your Way Into a New World

Every great fantasy story begins with a question. It's rarely something practical like "What's the weather today in this imaginary kingdom?" and more often something full of wonder, mystery, and possibility. It's a "What if...?" question. That question is the key to opening doors into brand-new worlds that never existed before you imagined them. And with ChatGPT by your side, these questions don't just lead to a single answer—they unlock hundreds of branching paths. Fantasy thrives on that kind of boundless creativity, and prompts are your magic spells to summon it.

The beauty of writing with ChatGPT is that you can experiment wildly. You're not limited to what you already know or can come up with in a single sitting. You can ask, "What if the moon were a giant sentient being who could only communicate with dreams?" and instantly get a scene idea, a character, a setting, or a full plot structure. That's the power of a single prompt. It doesn't just answer your question—it builds on it. The key is knowing how to ask.

Start by thinking in terms of cause and effect. Most fantasy worlds don't follow the same rules as ours, and they don't have to. In fact, they shouldn't. They should have their own rules, shaped by a different history, a different relationship with nature or time or death. Try questions like, *What if time flowed backward for an entire kingdom?* or *What if every lie told created a visible mark on the speaker's skin?* Instantly, you have tension. You have atmosphere. You have the seeds of a story.

And you don't have to stop at the big, cosmic-level ideas. You can prompt for personal stories that still feel deeply magical. *What if a baker discovers their bread has started granting people visions of the future?* or *What if a child finds a book that writes back?* These kinds of questions lead to fantasy stories that feel intimate and character-driven, perfect for short stories or screenplays with a strong emotional core.

You can also use the "What if...?" method to build layers into your story. Once you have a premise, ask more questions. *What if the kingdom the hero protects is built on a lie? What if the sword they wield hungers for the blood of the innocent as much as the guilty? What if the villain truly believes they're the hero?* With each prompt, you deepen the world, complicate the characters, and enrich the themes. It becomes less about magic for magic's sake and more about meaning, conflict, and transformation.

Fantasy readers love discovering new rules and systems that make the world tick. Use prompts to explore those systems. Ask, *What if magic came from emotion rather than spells?* or *What if the more powerful a mage became, the more of their memory they lost?* Now you've got a magic system with stakes and personal consequences. Ask ChatGPT to build out how that system works. You'll be amazed at the depth you can get with just a few questions and follow-ups.

One fun technique is to mash genres or tropes together using prompts. Say you're bored of traditional medieval fantasy. Try, *What if a cyberpunk city grew around the fossilized bones of a dragon, and the dragon wasn't quite dead?* Now you're exploring fantasy with tech. Or ask, *What if a romance bloomed between a demon and a healer during a holy war?* Boom—fantasy and love in high-stakes conflict. The collision of unexpected genres creates new kinds of fantasy that stand out.

You can also ask ChatGPT to give you full "What if" idea batches to pick from. Try: *Give me ten "what if" fantasy ideas involving lost civilizations* or *what if" questions about magical weather.* This shotgun method throws all sorts of ideas at you, and even if none are perfect, they often spark your own imagination. You'll start refining them, combining them, building stories in your head just by reading.

Another great use of "What if" is to flip a common trope. Fantasy is full of familiar story patterns—the chosen one, the evil overlord, the prophecy, the quest. But what if the chosen one was chosen by accident? What if the evil overlord was protecting the world from a worse threat? What if the prophecy had already happened and no one noticed? When you take something familiar and twist it, readers perk up. You've entered a world that feels fresh, even if its bones are old.

And don't forget tone. Your "What if" doesn't have to be epic or serious. It can be funny, weird, or cozy. *What if a tavern owner found out her ale could summon ghosts? What if an entire village was cursed to speak only in limericks?* These kinds of ideas are perfect for lighter fantasy, but they still offer narrative possibilities and unexpected turns. ChatGPT is surprisingly good at leaning into any tone you request—whimsy, horror, melancholy, satire—so your prompt can carry personality, not just plot.

Once you have your "What if" scenario, the next step is to explore it deeply. Ask ChatGPT to expand it into a scene, describe the setting, invent characters who live in that world, suggest conflicts that arise from the rules you just created. Don't stop at the surface. Keep prompting. Keep building. Each time you ask a question, you refine your new world and bring it into sharper focus.

Fantasy is, at its core, the art of asking bold questions and answering them in even bolder ways. The "What if" prompt is your spell. It's your invitation to wander through gates that no one else sees, into worlds that never existed until now. With ChatGPT acting as your guide and your sounding board, those worlds become easier to find and quicker to shape. You're not waiting around for inspiration to strike—you're striking sparks all over the place, knowing one of them will light the fire.

So go ahead. Ask the weird question. Follow the strange idea. Prompt your way into a story no one's ever told before. You'll be amazed where one sentence can take you.

And now that you've got a world beginning to form, let's dig into what makes your hero worth following through it.

Starting with the End: Writing Backwards with Purpose

One of the most powerful ways to write a fantasy story quickly and confidently is to begin at the end. That might sound backward, but it's actually a secret weapon—especially when time is limited. When you know where your story is going, it's easier to decide how to get there. You waste less time wondering what happens next, and instead, you focus your energy on making every scene serve the destination. It gives your story shape, direction, and a sense of inevitability. And when you're using ChatGPT to co-create, working backwards is like giving your magical writing assistant a treasure map.

Let's say you start with a simple idea: your protagonist defeats the villain and saves the realm. That's an ending, sure, but not a very specific one. The trick is to dig deeper. How does your protagonist win? What's the cost? What has changed in them or the world? Are they a better person, or have they sacrificed something essential? These details make your ending feel real and earned—and they give you clues about what your story needs to build up to that moment.

You could decide that your hero dies defeating the villain, but their actions awaken a new age of peace. Or maybe they survive, but the price is the loss of their magic, their love, or their identity. Maybe they win by making a truce rather than a kill. Maybe the villain is their long-lost sibling. Or the real villain was their mentor. Every ending comes with emotional weight, and once you've chosen it, everything else you write can aim toward it like a guided arrow.

This is where ChatGPT becomes especially useful. Once you've chosen your ending—or even a vague idea of it—you can prompt the AI to work backwards with you. Try something like: *"Help me plot a story where the protagonist sacrifices their memories to imprison a god."* Or *"I want the story to end with the hero realizing they were the villain all along—how can I structure the build-up to that twist?"* These kinds of prompts let ChatGPT reverse-engineer the journey with you. It can suggest key scenes, pivotal reveals, and character transformations that naturally lead to your chosen outcome.

This reverse approach also helps you resist the temptation to wander. Fantasy writers love to explore—and that's a good thing—but when you're writing a story in one day, you need focus. Knowing the ending helps you decide which characters are necessary, what scenes move the plot forward, and which parts are just shiny distractions. You don't have time to explore ten subplots or build a hundred kingdoms. You need to climb the mountain, not build new ones.

You can also use the ending to create your story's emotional core. Ask yourself: what feeling do you want the reader to walk away with? Awe? Sadness? Satisfaction? Hope? Then ask ChatGPT to help you reverse-engineer scenes that create those feelings. If you want the ending to be bittersweet, you'll need moments of beauty and loss throughout. If you want it to be triumphant, you'll need trials that make the victory feel earned. Try prompts like: *"Suggest scenes that lead to a tragic but heroic ending,"* or *"What character choices would make a hopeful ending more powerful?"*

Knowing your ending early also makes your magic systems, world-building, and plot devices easier to design. If your story ends with a kingdom breaking free from a magical curse, you can plant early clues about how the curse works, who created it, and why it's so hard to break. If your story ends with a character choosing peace over vengeance, you can structure their journey to test that choice again and again. The result is a story that feels tight and intentional—even if it was written in a day.

This method even works for stories that want to surprise the reader. You can plan a twist ending first, then ask ChatGPT to help you disguise it until the right moment. Let's say the twist is that the villain is actually trying to save the world from a greater threat. You can build your plot with clues hidden in plain sight. Ask ChatGPT for ideas: *"What are some subtle ways to hint that the villain is secretly good?"* or *"How can I make the reader rethink everything in the final chapter?"* Fantasy readers love these kinds of turns, and working backward makes them easier to execute well.

When your story has a strong ending, it also gives your characters stronger arcs. The protagonist's growth should reflect the journey they've taken. If they start off selfish and end up selfless, you can design scenes that push them through those changes. If they start off as a nobody and rise to lead a kingdom, you can build the moments where they gain respect, lose confidence, rise again, and finally take the crown. Ask ChatGPT to help fill in the gaps: *"What events could force this character to grow into a reluctant leader?"* or *"What trials would prepare this character to face their greatest fear in the final battle?"*

Even your setting can be built with the ending in mind. If the climax takes place on the crumbling cliffs of a forgotten temple, that place needs to be introduced earlier—maybe through legends, glimpses in dreams, or whispered warnings. If the final confrontation is between a hero and their corrupted former friend, you need scenes of closeness before the betrayal. ChatGPT can help you thread these moments in early, so they feel like destiny rather than convenience.

The best part of starting with the end is how much pressure it takes off the middle. You're not fumbling in the dark—you're lighting beacons along the way. Each one points toward your final scene, and as you write, the tension builds with purpose. The story begins to feel like a journey that couldn't end any other way. That's when readers lean in, and that's when you, the writer, feel like you're in full control—even when writing fast.

So when you sit down to write your fantasy story today, don't ask "Where do I begin?" Instead, ask "Where does it all end?" Let ChatGPT help you build the path from there. You'll be surprised how quickly the fog clears when you know what's waiting on the mountaintop.

And now that you've got the ending in sight, let's bring in the character who's going to walk that path—the hero your readers will root for, fear for, and never forget.

The Hero Is Everything: Designing Your Central Character

In fantasy, the world can be vast, the magic can be wild, and the stakes can be cosmic—but none of it matters if your hero doesn't grab the reader's attention. Your central character is the lens through which the reader experiences your story. Whether they're wielding a sword, casting forbidden spells, or simply trying to survive in a strange and magical land, their journey is what makes the fantasy feel real. You don't need a perfect character—you need one with drive, flaws, heart, and something to fight for. And when you're writing a story in a single day, getting your hero right from the start makes everything else fall into place more naturally.

Designing your hero with ChatGPT is like stepping into a hall of mirrors, each one reflecting a slightly different version of the character you might create. It's a fast, flexible way to explore different paths until one stands out. You can start with a broad request like, *"Give me a fantasy hero who is secretly descended from dragons,"* or *"Invent a protagonist who begins the story as a coward but ends it as a leader."* The AI will hand you a sketch, and you can instantly start playing with the details. Add a tragic backstory. Change their appearance. Twist their motivation. You're sculpting, not building from scratch.

At the heart of every compelling hero is a contradiction. That's what gives them depth. They might be brave but emotionally guarded, powerful but haunted by past failures, born noble but ashamed of their lineage. Ask ChatGPT to help you brainstorm those inner conflicts. Try prompts like, *"Give me a list of character flaws that would challenge a heroic journey,"* or *"Describe a fantasy hero who fears their own magical abilities."* These tensions create room for growth—and growth is what makes a character arc satisfying.

Don't forget that your hero needs something to want. This is their goal—the quest, the mission, the burning desire that pulls them through every obstacle. But underneath that, they also need something deeper they don't even know they're searching for. Maybe they think they want revenge, but what they really need is forgiveness. Maybe they're chasing glory but aching for love. These layered motivations make their journey rich and resonant. You can ask ChatGPT to help map these layers: *"What's a secret need that could conflict with a hero's public goal?"* You'll get ideas you hadn't even considered.

Another key part of designing your hero is thinking about where they start and where they end up. You already have the ending in mind, so now you can reverse-engineer the character arc. If your protagonist ends the story as a fearless protector of their people, where do they need to begin? Maybe they're a self-doubting exile who's afraid to lead. Ask ChatGPT to fill in the stages of transformation. *"What events would turn a reluctant loner into a brave leader?"* These beats give your story structure and emotional flow.

Fantasy heroes also need a strong visual presence. This helps not only with description but with reader connection. What does your hero look like? What do they wear? Do they carry a unique item or bear a mysterious mark? Do they have a physical trait that reveals something about their past or magic—silver eyes, flame-touched hair, a missing hand replaced by enchanted crystal? Ask ChatGPT for visual inspiration: *"Describe a fantasy hero with a unique and symbolic appearance."* You'll get sparks that help you write scenes full of imagery and impact.

Don't forget their voice. Readers fall in love with characters through dialogue just as much as action. Is your hero witty and sarcastic? Quiet and wise? Fiery and impulsive? Ask for a sample monologue or a few lines of dialogue to test how they sound. *"Write a short speech from a battle-weary hero refusing to give up."* You'll quickly feel whether the voice fits or needs tuning. You can refine it from there.

Relationships are also critical. Even the most powerful hero needs others to push against, learn from, or be wounded by. Think about the supporting cast: the mentor who trains them, the rival who challenges them, the friend who believes in them, the love interest who complicates everything. Ask ChatGPT to help you design these characters around your hero. *"Give me a loyal companion who balances out a reckless protagonist,"* or *"Create a mentor who's secretly working against the hero."* The hero's relationships often bring the deepest growth—and the best drama.

Another trick that works beautifully with ChatGPT is asking for backstory. You can prompt it like this: *"Create a backstory for a hero who was raised by thieves and now must protect the kingdom from invasion."* You'll be surprised at how much detail you get—childhood events, early betrayals, life-changing moments. You can use these to inform their reactions, decisions, and fears in the present. And if something doesn't fit, you can revise instantly. You're in full creative control, but you're never stuck or slowed down.

And finally, make sure your hero has something to lose. Stakes matter. Without them, the magic feels hollow. Ask yourself what would devastate your protagonist—and then make them risk it. Love, family, identity, purpose, home. Even in a fast-written story, these emotional stakes give your hero's journey weight. Ask ChatGPT, *"What could a hero lose in a battle that isn't just their life?"* or *"What inner belief might they have to sacrifice to win?"* These are the turning points where the reader gets goosebumps—and where you start feeling that this isn't just a fast story, but a good one.

The hero is the heart of your fantasy tale. Get them right, and everything else—the world, the plot, the magic—starts to come alive in service of their journey. And the best part is, you don't have to do it alone. ChatGPT is ready to help you sculpt a hero who's unforgettable, layered, and uniquely yours.

Now that your hero has taken shape, it's time to turn your attention to the dark side of the path—the force they must overcome, fear, or possibly even become. Let's create the villain.

Creating Antagonists worth Battling

If your hero is the heartbeat of your fantasy story, the antagonist is the storm that threatens it. They're not just the villain with a dark cloak and an evil laugh—they're the reason your protagonist grows, the source of the story's tension, and often the most unforgettable part of the journey. A strong antagonist forces your hero to question everything, to dig deeper, to risk more. And when you're writing a fantasy story in one day, having a powerful, well-defined antagonist gives your narrative energy and direction right from the start.

The best antagonists aren't just bad for the sake of being bad. They have purpose. Belief. Goals. They think they're right—or at least justified. When you use ChatGPT to build your villain, you're not just saying, "Make me a bad guy." You're saying, "Create someone who could've been the hero in another version of this story." That perspective shift is where the magic happens.

Start by deciding what kind of threat your antagonist represents. Are they a personal enemy, like a jealous sibling or a betrayed mentor? Are they a political force, like a tyrannical queen or a corrupt religious order? Are they something otherworldly—a demon, a god, a sentient storm, a cursed forest that wants to reclaim the land? You can prompt ChatGPT with something simple, like: *"Give me a fantasy villain who once saved the world but is now destroying it,"* or *"Create a magical being who feeds off broken promises."* You'll be surprised at how quickly a rich, layered character emerges.

Every great antagonist believes in something. Maybe they want order in a chaotic world. Maybe they're trying to undo a terrible mistake. Maybe they think they're the chosen one and your hero is just in the way. Ask ChatGPT: *"What might a villain believe that makes their actions feel justified?"* You'll get a list of motivations that you can match to your story's themes—control, revenge, sacrifice, legacy. These motivations help you write a villain who feels grounded, complex, and believable.

It's also helpful to think about how your villain reflects your hero. Often, they are two sides of the same coin. If your protagonist is trying to save the world through compassion and sacrifice, maybe the villain is trying to save it through domination and fear. They both want peace—but their methods are completely opposed. This creates not just conflict, but philosophical tension. Ask ChatGPT: *"Give me a villain who is a dark mirror of a hero who values freedom above all else."* These kinds of relationships add serious depth to your story.

A good antagonist needs presence. They don't just pop up in the final chapter with a lightning bolt and a monologue. You want their shadow to stretch across the whole story. Even if they're not physically there, their influence should be felt. Their laws. Their magic. Their soldiers. Their curse. Ask ChatGPT to help: *"What are ways to show the antagonist's power without them being in every scene?"* You might get ideas like blood-red banners flying across cities, whispers in the tavern about a dark ritual, or the hero discovering a burned village left as a warning.

Villains are also more memorable when they have personality. Sure, they can be cruel or cold, but they can also be charming, funny, seductive, bitter, calculating. Maybe they used to be your hero's friend, or maybe they're the hero's ancestor.

Try prompting: *"Describe a charismatic villain with a soft voice and deadly intentions,"* or *"Invent a villain who uses kindness to manipulate others."* These characters get under your skin—and your reader's too.

Don't be afraid to give your antagonist vulnerabilities. Maybe they're dying and desperate. Maybe they lost someone they loved and now want to burn the world in their grief. Maybe their power comes at a terrible price they can barely afford to keep paying. A flawed villain feels human, even if they're not human at all. Ask ChatGPT: *"What is a weakness that makes a powerful villain feel tragic?"* When your antagonist is as emotionally complicated as your hero, your story becomes much more than a good-versus-evil battle—it becomes a moral maze.

You can even make the antagonist *right.* At least in part. Maybe the world really is broken. Maybe the hero is naïve. Maybe the villain's actions, while cruel, are solving a problem no one else will face. These morally gray areas make your fantasy feel fresh and unpredictable. Ask ChatGPT for ideas like: *"Give me a villain who wants to destroy magic because it causes suffering,"* or *"What if the villain's goal is to unite the kingdoms, but through conquest?"* You'll start to see the antagonist not just as an obstacle, but as a storyteller in their own right.

Visually, your villain should be as memorable as your hero. Think iconic. Unique. Ask for inspiration: *"Describe the appearance of a villain who rules from a floating throne made of bones,"* or *"What does a villain look like who has been cursed to never speak but always be heard?"* These details make scenes more vivid and your antagonist more unforgettable.

And finally, make sure your antagonist pushes your hero to grow. They should create the pressure that forges the hero's change. Every encounter, every obstacle, every betrayal should reveal something new about both characters. You want their final confrontation to feel like the natural conclusion of everything that came before—not just a fight, but a collision of ideologies, emotions, and consequences.

In a one-day writing sprint, a great antagonist helps keep the pace sharp and the stakes high. And with ChatGPT, you can explore dozens of villain variations in minutes until you find the one that crackles with electricity.

Once you've created your antagonist, you've got both poles of the story's magnet. Now it's time to connect them with a journey worth taking—an adventure that tests, transforms, and transports. Let's step into the hero's path and explore the Hero's Journey through the lens of fast, effective storytelling.

The Hero's Journey in Fantasy: A Template with a Twist

If there's one structure that has guided more fantasy stories than any other, it's the Hero's Journey. It's the time-honoured arc that moves a character from the safety of their ordinary world into a realm of danger, transformation, and triumph. It's Frodo leaving the Shire. It's Harry stepping into Diagon Alley. It's the farm boy becoming a knight, the thief becoming a legend, the nobody becoming the saviour. The Hero's Journey is the backbone of fantasy—and when you're writing a story in a single day, it's the ultimate template for speed and power. But here's the fun part: once you know the pattern, you get to twist it, bend it, break it, and make it your own.

Let's start with the basics. The classic Hero's Journey is broken into stages: the call to adventure, refusal of the call, meeting the mentor, crossing the threshold, tests and trials, facing the abyss, transformation, and the return home. These aren't rigid rules—they're signposts. You don't need to include every one, and you don't need to hit them in order. What matters is that the journey *feels* like a journey. That your hero changes because of what they go through.

When you're using ChatGPT to write fast, the Hero's Journey becomes a framework you can lean on. You can prompt it with something like: *"Outline a fantasy story using the Hero's Journey where the protagonist is a cursed oracle,"* or *"Give me a Hero's Journey structure for a thief who steals a magical relic and awakens an ancient evil."* In seconds, you'll have a rough arc with beats you can fill in, expand, and customize.

But the real power lies in the twist.

Fantasy is at its most exciting when it surprises the reader, even while following a familiar path. So ask yourself—how can I take the Hero's Journey and flip it? What if the mentor is actually the villain? What if the hero crosses the threshold, but wants to go back immediately and can't? What if the journey never ends, and the story ends with the hero refusing to return home? These reversals keep the reader on their toes, and they keep *you*, the writer, engaged.

Let's say you've got a basic Hero's Journey plotted out with ChatGPT. You can now prompt for unusual variations: *"Give me alternative trials for a hero who can't use violence,"* or *"Describe a magical realm where the journey physically ages the traveler with each step."* Suddenly, your journey has new texture. It's not just about getting from point A to point B—it's about what happens to the hero along the way, and how it challenges everything they thought they knew.

You can also use the Hero's Journey to shape your worldbuilding. Each phase of the journey can introduce a new part of your fantasy world. The "tests and trials" phase is perfect for magical forests, treacherous ruins, or mysterious allies. The "abyss" is where the world should feel most strange and dangerous. Maybe magic itself breaks down. Maybe time runs backward. Maybe the hero must face a vision of their own death. Ask ChatGPT to design those places: *"Describe the landscape the hero must cross to reach the Temple of Forgotten Names,"* or *"Give me a scene where the hero meets a twisted version of themselves."*

Emotionally, the Hero's Journey gives you a great arc to work with in a short story or novella. In the beginning, the hero is incomplete. In the middle, they're tested. At the end, they're changed—wounded, wiser, stronger, or broken in a way that feels earned. Use prompts like *"What emotional breakthroughs can a hero experience during their journey?"* or *"How can I show the hero's internal transformation through physical actions?"* This keeps your story grounded even when the world is filled with magic and mayhem.

You can also focus on the relationships that change across the journey. The friend who becomes a rival. The stranger who becomes a soulmate. The enemy who becomes an uneasy ally. Ask ChatGPT: *"Give me relationship arcs that follow the Hero's Journey,"* and you'll find ways to layer complexity into your story without needing massive subplots. These emotional beats give your fantasy story warmth and gravity.

Now, if you're writing with speed in mind, don't feel like you have to spend hours plotting every step. Think of the Hero's Journey like a road with eight major stops. You know where it begins and where it ends. The stops in between—those can be flexible. If your hero starts in a place of comfort, you know they'll have to leave it. If they gain power, they'll also have to suffer loss. If they're running from something, they'll eventually have to face it. You don't need every answer—you just need the compass.

Twisting the Hero's Journey also means twisting the roles. What if your protagonist isn't the true hero, but just the decoy? What if the journey belongs to a group rather than one person? What if the hero fails, and it's in that failure that the world is truly saved? You can challenge the shape of the journey and still make it feel satisfying. Try prompts like *"Show me a fantasy story where the Hero's Journey ends in ambiguity,"* or *"Write a version of the Hero's Journey where each stage is completed by a different character."* These variations give your fantasy story a sense of freshness, even when built on familiar bones.

And the Hero's Journey doesn't have to be epic. It can be small and personal. Maybe the "return home" is a literal return to a village after a traumatic event. Maybe the "abyss" is a confrontation with a parent. Maybe the "boon" the hero gains isn't power or treasure—but forgiveness. When you let emotion guide the journey instead of just spectacle, your fantasy becomes timeless.

In a one-day writing sprint, using the Hero's Journey is like riding a well-trained dragon—you've got a sense of where it's going, but you can still feel the thrill of the flight. And with ChatGPT as your co-pilot, you can soar through scenes, generate ideas for each stage, and adjust on the fly without losing momentum.

So grab your map. Choose your twist. And get your hero ready to cross that threshold. Their journey is about to begin—and your story is about to take off.

Next, let's focus on the setting: the magical, dangerous, and breathtaking world that makes fantasy... well, fantasy.

From Nothing to Kingdom: Building a Fantasy World in Minutes

Let's be honest—worldbuilding in fantasy can feel like a mountain too steep to climb, especially when you're trying to write a complete story in a single day. You might imagine hours lost to drawing maps, crafting histories, designing languages, and figuring out why the moons are purple and the mountains float. But here's the good news: you don't need all that up front. You just need *enough*. Enough to make the world feel real. Enough to give your characters room to breathe. Enough to create that feeling of stepping into a place unlike any other. And with ChatGPT, you can go from nothing to a living, breathing fantasy kingdom in minutes.

Start with a single spark. You don't need to build an entire continent. Just begin with a place. A city, a village, a forest, a desert fortress—something your character will interact with in the first few scenes. Ask ChatGPT: *"Describe a fantasy village hidden inside a giant tree,"* or *"Give me a desert city where water is currency."* You'll immediately get textures, customs, and visuals to anchor your story. That's your foundation.

Once you have a location, ask: what's unusual about it? Fantasy thrives on difference. Maybe gravity works differently. Maybe the city floats. Maybe the mountains bleed when the earth is wounded. You can ask: *"What magical phenomena might affect a city built atop an ancient magical battlefield?"* With just a couple of follow-up prompts, you'll have traditions, superstitions, maybe even a calendar built around strange seasons or celestial events. But remember—don't go too deep. You're not designing a tabletop RPG campaign. You're building a world for one story, right now.

Next, focus on society. Who lives here? What kinds of beings walk the streets—humans, elves, talking animals, stone-skinned giants, sentient shadows? What's their relationship with one another? Is the kingdom ruled by a benevolent monarch, or is it a council of corrupted high priests who manipulate time? Try prompts like: *"Describe the political structure of a kingdom where magic is outlawed,"* or *"What kind of government might exist in a city built by dragons and inherited by humans?"* The AI will generate fascinating dynamics you can immediately weave into your plot.

Magic is the lifeblood of most fantasy worlds, so you'll want to establish its rules. Not all the rules—just the core ones. Who can use magic? How does it work? What does it cost? Ask ChatGPT: *"Create a unique magic system based on memory,"* or *"What are the risks of using blood magic in a kingdom where it's forbidden?"* The answers you get can directly shape your characters' challenges and decisions. A world where magic drains your life force is instantly more dramatic than one where it's free and unlimited.

Your fantasy world also needs history—but not in an encyclopedia-entry kind of way. Think scars. What happened in the past that still echoes in the present? Was there a great war, a cataclysm, a betrayal that shattered the kingdoms? Ask: *"What ancient event shaped the borders of a fractured magical empire?"* or *"Describe a long-lost civilization whose ruins still hum with forgotten power."* These backdrops provide tension and mystery without requiring you to write a thousand years of fictional history.

Now layer in culture. What do people believe in this world? Are the gods distant and silent, or do they walk among mortals? Are there festivals, taboos, rites of passage? Ask ChatGPT: *"Invent a religious belief system for a culture that worships the moon as a living being,"* or *"Describe the coming-of-age ceremony in a tribe that bonds with elemental spirits."* These cultural details enrich your scenes, create world-specific dialogue, and deepen character motivations.

You can also go smaller—think about food, clothing, currency, slang. What do people eat in the mountain cities? What do street merchants shout in the bustling markets? What insult do people throw at someone who breaks sacred tradition? Ask for worldbuilding tidbits like: *"What kinds of food might be sold in a floating city's bazaar?"* or *"Give me three slang terms used by smugglers in an outlaw kingdom."* These elements make your fantasy world feel lived-in without overloading your word count.

When worldbuilding with ChatGPT, one of the most powerful tricks is to build just-in-time. You don't need to know what the underwater cities look like unless your hero goes there. You don't need to know the name of the mountain god unless someone's praying to it. Ask for what you need, when you need it. You can always expand later. This just-in-time method keeps your writing fast, fluid, and focused on the story.

The tone of your world matters, too. Is this a dark, brooding land where hope flickers like candlelight? Or is it a whimsical, colorful place where the sky rains sugar and skeletons tell bedtime stories? Ask ChatGPT to help capture the tone: *"Describe a whimsical fantasy world full of gentle oddities,"* or *"Create a bleak, cursed landscape shaped by ancient sorrow."* The tone will help shape your descriptions, dialogue, and even the way your characters view the world around them.

Another tip: connect your world to your characters. Don't worldbuild in isolation. If your protagonist is a thief, ask what the underground criminal network looks like. If your villain is a banished priestess, ask how the temple hierarchy works. Every time you build the world through the eyes of a character, it becomes more personal and easier to write.

And finally, don't stress about being original. All fantasy borrows from something. The trick is to twist it. Add your spin. Ask ChatGPT to help you remix old tropes: *"Give me a fresh take on elves,"* or *"Reimagine dragons as metaphysical forces instead of creatures."* The goal isn't to reinvent the genre—it's to make a world that feels exciting and real to you, right now.

By the end of an hour, you can have a kingdom, a culture, a conflict, and a map in your head—without ever drawing one. It doesn't take years. It doesn't even take days. With ChatGPT as your magical architect, you can build a world in minutes that's rich enough to host a compelling fantasy tale. And once the world is ready, the story can finally breathe within it.

Naming Your World, Its People, and Its Wonders

Names matter more than people realize. In fantasy, names do more than label places and characters—they shape tone, hint at history, and pull readers deeper into your world. A name can evoke wonder, dread, elegance, mystery. It can sound ancient and sacred, or fresh and strange. And when you're writing a fantasy story in one day, it's easy to fall into the trap of filler names like "Kingdom A" or "The Evil Forest." That's where ChatGPT becomes your enchanted name forger, turning blank spaces into places that feel alive with story.

Let's start with the name of your world. This is the stage where everything unfolds. You want something evocative, but not distracting. Something that feels like it could belong on a map, whispered in old songs or etched into crumbling scrolls. Try asking ChatGPT: *"Give me ten names for a fantasy world torn apart by elemental magic,"* or *"What's a good name for a mystical realm floating between dimensions?"* You'll get lists with different flavors—some harsh and jagged, others lyrical and mysterious. Don't be afraid to tweak what the AI gives you. Combine syllables, reverse words, or take two and mash them together. What matters most is that *you* feel the name fits the tone of your tale.

Once you have the world, zoom in. What's the name of the city where your hero begins their journey? Is it a place of secrets or celebration? Ruins or power? Again, ask for help based on the vibe: *"Name a fortress city built into the cliffs of a forgotten sea,"* or *"Suggest a name for a moonlit elven village hidden in the trees."* ChatGPT will usually give you names that carry weight—names that sound like they have stories buried inside them.

And don't stop at cities. Name regions, mountains, rivers, forests, and deserts. These names can add atmosphere fast. *The Thornweld. The Glass Mire. Ashfall Peaks. The Spirelands.* You don't need to go full Tolkien and name everything, but a few well-placed names make your world feel expansive and immersive. Ask ChatGPT for a list of options for each environment as you write. You don't have to plan it all up front—you can name as you go.

Now let's talk about people. Your characters' names carry culture, personality, and even fate. The name of a high priestess shouldn't sound the same as that of a street thief. Ask ChatGPT: *"Give me a list of noble-sounding names for a magical bloodline,"* or *"Create rough, clipped names for a desert-dwelling warrior tribe."* You can even base naming conventions on language rules—like ending all feminine names with "-ya" or giving royal houses Latin-sounding roots. It's a subtle trick that makes your cultures feel consistent, even if they're just implied.

Titles and nicknames are also huge in fantasy. A character might be called *The Nightless Queen*, *He Who Walks Between*, *The Bone Merchant*, or *Ashborn*. These titles often do more than just sound cool—they suggest history, danger, or mystery. Ask ChatGPT: *"Give me five mysterious titles for a villain who manipulates dreams,"* or *"What might a hero be called after defeating a god?"* These monikers add depth instantly and can be woven into your dialogue, folklore, or chapter headings for flavor.

Magical artifacts, legendary creatures, and mystical locations need names, too. The more specific you get in your prompt, the more fitting the results. Ask: *"What would a cursed sword forged in dragonfire be called?"* or *"Name a sea monster worshiped by islanders as a god."* You'll get dramatic, evocative results like *The Emberfang*, *Whispermaw*, *The Oathbreaker's Crown*, or *The Hollow Heart*. Use these to create the sense that your world is full of legend, myth, and danger—even if you only touch on them in the story.

One of the best ways to make your names feel authentic is to build loose naming systems for different cultures or species in your world. If the forest elves use flowing, vowel-rich names, while the mountain clans speak in gruff, consonant-heavy terms, you've already created a linguistic divide that helps readers distinguish your peoples quickly. Ask

ChatGPT: *"Create naming conventions for a seafaring nation inspired by Norse and Polynesian cultures,"* and it'll give you root words, suffixes, and sound patterns you can reuse throughout your story.

You can also play with hidden meanings. Names that contain hints about a character's destiny or the truth of a place are especially satisfying in fantasy. Maybe the city of *Vel'thir* translates to "veiled truth" in an ancient tongue. Maybe your villain's real name has been forgotten, replaced by a title that conceals their origin. Ask for meanings when you generate names: *"Give me ten names for an ancient sword, each with a secret meaning,"* or *"Create the name of a mountain that once housed a forgotten god."* You'll find layers of subtext that enrich your story without slowing you down.

Sometimes, you don't even need a full backstory—just the right name can tell a whole tale. A bar called *The One-Eyed Cat* feels like it has stories to tell. A ruin known as *The Dagger Grave* suggests betrayal and ancient bloodshed. A creature called *Skeltrune* already feels like it's lurking in shadows. You can create this atmosphere instantly using ChatGPT: *"Name a pub in a cursed town,"* or *"What would villagers call a haunted lake that sings at night?"*

As you write, keep a small running list of the names you're using. Not for obsessive tracking, but just to avoid repetition and keep things coherent. With ChatGPT helping you generate new ones on the fly, you'll never get stuck calling your third village "Old Town" again.

In fantasy, a name is never just a name. It's a spell. A symbol. A promise that this world you're writing matters. And you don't need hours of etymology or years of linguistic study to make it feel right. You just need the right prompt, a little instinct, and a willingness to follow what sounds true.

So name your world. Name your people. Name the forgotten places and the creatures that guard them. With every name, you're building something real.

And once the names are echoing through your story like ancient wind through the trees, it's time to take a walk through your world's terrain. Let's talk about maps, landscapes, and how to make geography serve your plot.

Maps in the Mind: Visualizing Fantasy Geography with Prompts

Fantasy and maps go hand in hand. Even if you never sketch a single coastline or label a single mountain range, your story still needs geography. Readers want to feel the terrain beneath their feet, smell the damp of the enchanted forest, see the glow of a distant tower across a desert of glass. Geography in fantasy isn't just about where things are—it's about how the world moves, breathes, divides, and connects. It's about creating the feeling that this world extends far beyond the borders of your story. The good news is, you don't need to draw anything at all. With ChatGPT, you can build detailed mental maps using prompts that create geography rich with story potential.

Start by imagining the journey. Most fantasy stories involve movement. The hero leaves somewhere and ends up somewhere else—emotionally, physically, often both. Ask yourself: what kind of terrain lies between the beginning and the end? If your story starts in a quiet village and ends in the ruins of a god-temple, what would make that path interesting? Dangerous? Magical? Now ask ChatGPT: *"Create a list of fantasy locations between a remote mountain village and a cursed forest at the edge of the world."* You'll get a journey filled with cliffs, bridges, riverlands, war zones, and ancient cities swallowed by sand. Each one is a possible setting for a scene.

Geography isn't just filler. It creates story by creating *obstacles*. Mountains must be climbed. Swamps must be crossed. Canyons must be bridged. Fantasy geography should challenge your characters. A desert isn't just hot—it's filled with mirages, hidden tombs, sandstorms, and nomadic tribes. A forest isn't just full of trees—it's alive, possibly sentient, maybe even carnivorous. Ask for depth: *"Describe a living forest that traps travelers in illusions,"* or *"What dangers might lurk in the floating islands above the Endless Sea?"* You're not building a place—you're building an experience.

Think about borders, too. Fantasy stories often revolve around kingdoms, realms, and empires. Ask: *Where do the boundaries lie, and why?* Are they political, magical, or carved into the land by some ancient catastrophe? Try prompts like: *"Describe a mountain range that divides two warring nations,"* or *"What kind of magical barrier could encircle a hidden valley?"* These boundaries aren't just visual—they represent tension, history, and often fear.

Climate plays a role in storytelling tone. If your hero is trudging through ice-covered tundra, the story feels bleak, harsh, and lonely. If they're hiking through lush jungle ruins lit by fireflies and bioluminescent vines, it feels mystical, rich, and full of secrets. Ask ChatGPT: *"Describe the terrain and climate of a kingdom built on volcanic rock,"* or *"Give me the weather patterns of a coastal empire ruled by storm sorcerers."* These prompts give you descriptions to use instantly in your story—and you don't need to memorize or draw a thing.

You can also use geography to symbolize character journeys. A rising mountain can reflect personal growth. A descent into caverns can mirror emotional breakdown. A long desert crossing might echo a search for identity. With ChatGPT, you can even be poetic about it. Ask: *"What kind of landscape reflects a journey of grief and healing?"* or *"Create terrain that mirrors a character's fall from grace."* Fantasy worlds aren't just maps—they're metaphors waiting to happen.

Cities are geography, too. Don't just name them—shape them. Ask: *"Describe a city built into the bones of a dead god,"* or *"What does a mountaintop capital of cloud-walkers look like?"* The way cities are built tells readers about their culture, resources, and beliefs. A city of towers and skybridges might reflect a people who prize observation and distance. A city of tunnels and silence might speak to a past filled with hiding and fear. Each location is a chance to reveal history and personality.

And don't forget ruins. Fantasy is fueled by the past. Ancient cities. Forgotten roads. Lost temples half-swallowed by vines. Ask for evocative settings: *"Describe the remains of a fallen kingdom now haunted by magical echoes,"* or *"What might a sunken city look like when the tides recede during the eclipse?"* These places don't need long explanations—just enough visual weight to ground a scene or create a moment of awe.

You can also create travel tension using geography. If the only way across the continent is the Leviathan Bridge—an ancient, crumbling structure of magical bone—your characters are forced into danger. If the road splits between the cursed marsh and the cliff path known for bandits, you've got drama. Ask: *"Give me travel routes that force characters into difficult choices,"* or *"What's the most dangerous but fastest way through the Emerald Wilds?"* These become ready-made decisions for your characters, and scene gold for you as a writer.

Even fantasy maps have lore. Why is the sea called *The Widow's Wake*? Why is that forest labeled *Unspoken*? Why do locals refuse to climb *Howler's Peak* during the full moon? Ask ChatGPT for place-name lore: *"Invent legends surrounding five named locations on a fantasy map,"* and you'll get micro-stories embedded in the landscape. These are the kinds of details that make a reader feel like your world goes on, even beyond the page.

And when you *do* want to visualize a map, just do it in your mind. Walk your character from place to place. Describe the terrain as they travel. Feel how long it takes. Use ChatGPT as your compass: *"Describe the scenery a traveler sees when crossing from the salt plains into the Black Hollow."* You'll paint pictures in your prose even if there's no literal map on paper.

Geography in fantasy doesn't have to be a chore or a rabbit hole. It can be fast, expressive, and directly tied to your plot, characters, and themes. You're not worldbuilding for the sake of complexity—you're building the emotional and narrative paths your characters walk. And with prompts at your fingertips, you can create cliffs, valleys, rivers, and cities that feel just as real as your hero's choices.

Now that your world has shape and space, let's fill it with something mysterious and powerful—let's dive into the systems of magic that make fantasy so enchanting, unpredictable, and full of wonder.

Let's Talk Magic: Creating Your Own Rules of Power

Magic is what sets fantasy apart from every other genre. It's the sparkle in the air, the thunder in the blood, the impossible made real. But here's the thing—magic only works if it *feels* like it works. If it's too vague or too convenient, readers will check out. They'll roll their eyes when your hero escapes because "the amulet glowed" or "the spell worked just in time." Magic has to have rules. Boundaries. Cost. It can be wild and wondrous, but it still needs structure. That's what makes it matter. And when you're writing a fantasy story in one day, a solid magic system will help you write scenes faster, build tension quicker, and stay grounded in your world.

The best part is, you don't need a huge textbook of spells to make it happen. You just need a simple framework. And with ChatGPT, you can build that framework in minutes. All it takes is a few key questions—and a few prompts to help you answer them.

Start with this: **Where does the magic come from?** Is it divine? Elemental? Drawn from the land? The stars? Memories? Emotion? Blood? Music? Ask ChatGPT: *"Give me ideas for unique fantasy magic sources,"* and you'll get options like dreams, shadows, names, or even sorrow. Pick one that fits the tone of your world. If your setting is dark and twisted, maybe magic feeds on pain. If it's whimsical and strange, maybe magic is traded in riddles or laughter.

Next, ask: **Who can use it?** Is magic rare or common? Do only the elite have access? Is it inherited, studied, stolen, or stumbled upon? Ask for ideas like: *"How might a society control access to magic?"* or *"What kind of caste system might develop around magical ability?"* These answers help shape your world and the characters within it. A hero born powerless in a society ruled by spellcasters has a built-in struggle. A villain trying to hoard magic for their chosen few creates immediate stakes.

Then get into the **rules**. Magic needs limits. Can it only be used at night? Does it require a toll—like aging the caster, or taking a memory, or burning part of the soul? Maybe spells require rare ingredients, or exact gestures, or emotional clarity. Ask ChatGPT: *"Give me five limitations for a magic system based on elemental forces,"* or *"What are some consequences of using unstable magic?"* When magic has a cost, using it becomes a decision—not a shortcut.

Also think about **how** magic works in practice. Do people speak spells aloud? Use gestures? Tattoos? Scrolls? Potions? Do they need a wand, a relic, or simply focus of mind? Ask: *"Describe a magic system where emotions fuel spells,"* or *"Create a ritual for summoning light from ancient runes."* These visuals make your scenes come alive. They give your characters something physical to do, and your readers something vivid to imagine.

Magic should also **interact** with your world. How does it shape politics, religion, crime, warfare? If magic can bring someone back to life, is there a black market for resurrection? If healing magic exists, do normal doctors go out of business—or become the ones who treat magical injuries? Use prompts like: *"What would a city look like if teleportation magic were common?"* or *"Describe a religion formed around a magical storm that appears every century."* Suddenly, your magic isn't just a tool—it's woven into culture and belief.

And don't forget **conflict**. A great fantasy story often centers around who controls the magic, who's barred from it, and what happens when someone breaks the rules. Maybe your villain wants to tear down the magical order. Maybe your hero is using outlawed spells. Maybe the old magic is dying and something darker is rising to replace it. Ask ChatGPT: *"What political systems might form around magic that's running out?"* or *"How could a forbidden school of magic be rediscovered?"* These setups are gold for drama and plot.

If you want to add extra texture, build **different types of magic** within the same world. One region might use blood rites, while another uses song. One race of beings might cast through thought alone, while humans need elaborate rituals. Ask: *"Design regional variations of a magic system in a fantasy world,"* and you'll get layers you can use to create tension between cultures, allies, or characters.

Sometimes it's fun to base your magic on something totally original or unexpected. Cooking, architecture, knots, patterns, dreams. You could try: *"Give me a magic system where each spell is tied to a musical note,"* or *"Describe a world where magic is only accessible through forgotten languages."* These unique systems make your story stand out, even if it's short or written quickly.

Keep in mind that magic isn't just a plot device—it's also a **mirror**. It reflects the characters who wield it. A hero who can only use magic when they feel pure love is very different from one who grows more powerful the more hate they feel. A villain who needs to confess their sins before casting spells offers completely different story beats than one who draws strength from silence. Use prompts like: *"What does this magic system say about the user's personality or morality?"* and you'll find yourself writing scenes with emotional weight—not just flashy effects.

As you're writing, don't feel the need to explain everything up front. Let the reader experience magic the same way your characters do—through action, discovery, and consequence. If a character lights a torch by slicing their palm and whispering into the flame, the reader doesn't need to know *why* it works right away. Let it unfold. Use the mystery of magic to build suspense and deepen the story.

And finally, make sure that your magic system **feeds your story, not slows it down**. If your protagonist must master a forbidden spell to defeat the antagonist, that becomes a major plot point. If magic is what's tearing the world apart, make every spell a step closer to collapse. Ask ChatGPT to help you link magic to theme: *"How can a magic system based on truth reflect a story about identity?"* or *"How might a love story develop in a world where magic prevents lying?"*

In a single writing day, a strong, simple magic system can save you hours of uncertainty. It gives your plot direction, your characters power and conflict, and your world texture. With just a few prompts and the right questions, you can create magic that feels real—raw, wild, dangerous, beautiful.

And now that your world has power running through its veins, let's conjure the creatures, beasts, and ancient beings who haunt it, guide it, or threaten to tear it apart. Let's bring your fantasy world to life.

Magical Creatures: Breathing Life into Beasts and Beings

No fantasy world feels complete without its magical creatures. They slither in the shadows of forgotten ruins, soar across twilight skies, whisper secrets in lost languages, or wait in ancient woods with eyes older than memory. Some are allies, some are enemies, and some are forces of nature you don't dare define. These beasts and beings are more than set dressing—they bring wonder, danger, humor, and mystery to your story. And when you're writing a fantasy tale in a single day, they offer ready-made moments of awe, fear, or delight that deepen your world without slowing you down. With ChatGPT by your side, you can summon entire bestiaries in minutes.

The trick to magical creatures isn't complexity—it's specificity. You don't need a creature with ten paragraphs of biology. You need a creature that *feels* like it belongs. Something with a unique shape, a strange behavior, a symbolic presence. Start with a simple prompt like: *"Give me ten original magical creatures found in a haunted forest,"* and you'll get a flavorful list full of potential plot points. You can then pick one, ask for a detailed description, and build it into a scene where your hero is warned not to step on the moss that glows red—it means the *Lurksap* is near.

The first thing to consider is **function**. What does this creature do in your world—or more importantly, in your story? Is it a guardian, a predator, a companion, a divine messenger? Is it rare and revered, or common and annoying like a magical raccoon that steals enchanted trinkets? Ask ChatGPT: *"Create a magical creature that protects an ancient underground city,"* or *"What kind of magical pests might infest a wizard's tower?"* You'll get creatures that do more than just fill space—they drive scenes.

Another great angle is **symbolism**. Magical creatures often reflect themes or character arcs. A phoenix isn't just a bird—it's a symbol of rebirth. A shapeshifter might echo a hero's struggle with identity. A siren might tempt a character who fears losing control. You can ask ChatGPT for creatures based on emotion or theme: *"Invent a magical creature that represents regret,"* or *"Create a beast that feeds on lies."* These beings become metaphors that deepen your story even as they build your world.

You can also think in terms of **ecology**. Where does the creature live? What does it eat? How does it interact with the land, the weather, the people? Even just asking for this info gives you tons of narrative color. Try: *"Describe a high-altitude creature that lives on floating islands,"* or *"Give me a magical sea predator that lives in whirlpools."* Suddenly, you've got not just a creature—but a setting, a culture that fears or reveres it, maybe even a myth that shapes your hero's decisions.

Appearance matters, but it's not just about being cool-looking. What's *strange* about this creature? Does it walk backward? Speak in riddles? Cry gemstones? Shed its memories every moon? Ask ChatGPT for quirks: *"Give me five unusual behaviors for a forest-dwelling magical creature,"* or *"Invent a creature whose biology confuses even the most learned mages."* These quirks are what stick in a reader's mind. You want them to remember the time your hero faced a feathered lion that purrs illusions into your ears—not just a generic beast.

Some of the most powerful scenes in fantasy involve a creature that's misunderstood. Maybe it's feared, but it's actually lonely. Maybe it's ancient and wise, but bound by a curse. These beings make excellent side characters or even plot catalysts. Ask: *"Create a magical creature who once ruled a kingdom but now lives in exile,"* or *"Design a dragon who has lost the ability to breathe fire and hides from other dragons."* These aren't just beasts—they're characters with motivations and scars.

Creatures can also help you explore **myth and culture**. What do different groups in your world believe about them? Is the same beast seen as a god in one land and a demon in another? Are there festivals held to honor—or ward off—their return? Ask ChatGPT: *"Describe a festival held in honor of a creature that hasn't been seen in centuries,"* or *"What legends might exist about a serpent that sleeps beneath a kingdom's capital?"* You don't need to write all the lore—just enough to hint that the world stretches far beyond the frame of your story.

You can use creatures to create plot hooks, too. Maybe a village hires the hero to slay a monster—but the creature turns out to be intelligent and unjustly blamed. Maybe an ancient beast awakens as a side effect of someone casting a forbidden spell. Maybe the hero's fate is tied to a celestial being that appears once every hundred years. Ask: *"What creature might be accidentally awakened by a magical ritual gone wrong?"* or *"Give me a plot idea involving a cursed creature bound to the protagonist."* Now the creature isn't just background—it's part of the spine of your story.

Companions are another fun option. Not every magical being needs to be dangerous or distant. Some might be funny, loyal, awkward, or unexpectedly wise. The tiny winged lizard who hoards buttons. The melancholy ghost-dog who follows the hero from scene to scene. These companions can help with exposition, add comic relief, or even turn the tide of a major moment. Ask ChatGPT: *"Invent a magical sidekick creature who helps a hero in subtle, annoying ways,"* or *"Give me a creature who bonds with a character by sharing their dreams."* These little touches make your story memorable.

And when you want to push beyond the expected—dragons, unicorns, phoenixes—you can blend genres and ideas. Ask for mashups: *"What happens if a jellyfish evolves to feed on spell energy?"* or *"Describe a fungal hive-mind creature that grows memories like fruit."* These hybrid ideas will spark all kinds of plot threads and visual imagery.

Above all, keep your magical creatures purposeful. Whether they serve as metaphor, myth, mystery, or menace, make sure they move the story forward or deepen the world in a way that matters. Don't toss in a beast just to check a fantasy box. Let it *mean* something—even if it only appears in one scene.

With ChatGPT, you can fill your story with wonders you never could've come up with on your own in a single sitting. You'll have creatures that slither, fly, whisper, curse, heal, and haunt your characters long after the story ends.

Now that your world is inhabited by magic and mystery, let's shift our focus to the divine and the legendary—those beings and forces that shape belief systems, guide destinies, and rewrite fate. It's time to explore the gods, spirits, and mythologies of your world.

Gods, Spirits, and Mythologies: Inventing Fantasy Lore

If magic is the pulse of a fantasy world, then mythology is its soul. It's the echo of ancient stories whispered across generations, the reason people light candles at night, the names they curse when thunder rolls or stars fall. Gods, spirits, and legends don't just add color to your world—they shape its laws, culture, and conflict. And when you're writing a fantasy story in one day, lore gives your world gravity. It makes it feel like it's been around long before the first line of your story—and will continue long after the last.

You don't need to invent an entire pantheon to bring your fantasy world to life. One god, one myth, one spirit's curse—that's enough to build a whole story around. And with ChatGPT, you can spin entire belief systems from thin air in moments. You just need to ask the right questions, and let the answers breathe into your world.

Start with a simple prompt like: *"Invent a god of forgotten things,"* or *"Describe a trickster spirit who lives in moonlight."* What you'll get are personalities, symbols, rituals, and legends that feel like they've existed for centuries. You can ask for their domain—love, war, harvests, shadows, death—and ChatGPT will build from there. Suddenly, you have a force that the people in your world live with, fear, worship, or rebel against.

Next, consider how these gods or spirits interact with the world. Are they silent forces, or do they walk among mortals? Are they benevolent, vengeful, indifferent, or childlike? Some gods might demand sacrifices. Others might reward those who defy them. Some may have disappeared, leaving a vacuum of faith behind. Ask: *"What happens in a world where the gods went silent a thousand years ago?"* or *"Create a legend about a goddess who drowned her own temple to save her worshippers."* These story seeds can lead to side quests, major arcs, or even entire themes in your plot.

One of the best uses of mythology is to explain the unexplainable. Why does the river never freeze? Why is the moon always full in one part of the kingdom? Why is one village cursed with eternal night? The answers don't have to be logical—they have to *feel* true within your world. Ask ChatGPT: *"Invent a legend that explains why the stars vanish every ten years,"* or *"What folk tale might be told about a mountain that moans during storms?"* These little details create layers. Readers may never know every answer—but they'll sense the depth.

Your lore can also influence how people behave. If a god of death is feared, maybe burial rites are elaborate and sacred. If a spirit is believed to guard travelers, maybe every caravan leaves an offering of salt and stone at the crossroads. Ask: *"What rituals might a desert culture perform to honor a wind spirit?"* or *"Describe a wedding custom in a land devoted to a god of duality."* These cultural elements make scenes feel richer, even in fast-paced stories.

Don't forget myths that contradict. Just like in our own world, fantasy religions can have multiple versions of the same event. One people's saviour is another's destroyer. This makes your world feel alive with belief, argument, and mystery. Ask for complexity: *"Give me two opposing myths about the same event,"* or *"Create rival cults worshipping the same deity in different ways."* This opens the door to philosophical and political conflict—and great drama.

Spirits don't have to be divine to be meaningful. They can be local, elemental, or ancestral. Forest spirits who guide lost travelers. House spirits who protect homes but demand silence after sunset. Water spirits who can grant safe passage—but only once. Ask ChatGPT: *"Invent a mischievous spirit that lives in wells,"* or *"Describe an ancestral spirit bound to a family bloodline."* These beings can be allies, antagonists, or wildcards in your story.

Mythology also gives you built-in metaphors and motifs. A character born under the sign of the twin moons may be fated for duality. A kingdom whose founding myth involves a sword rising from the sea might have deep superstitions about water. You can thread this symbolism through your narrative for resonance. Ask: *"What legends might shape the values of a warrior society?"* or *"Describe a creation myth that inspires rebellion in a conquered people."* These layers turn simple conflicts into something epic.

And sometimes, the lore *is* the mystery. Maybe your story centers around a prophecy. Or the return of a forgotten god. Or the breaking of an ancient curse. Use prompts like: *"Create a prophecy that sounds noble but hides a dark truth,"* or *"What might be the lost name of a god erased from all written history?"* Suddenly, your fantasy tale has urgency—and the past becomes a force that can't be ignored.

You don't need to explain everything to the reader. Let some lore be implied, half-remembered, or questioned by the characters themselves. When the hero enters a ruined temple and says, "They say this place was built for the god of lies," you don't need to tell the whole story—just that whisper of myth changes the air in the scene.

Fantasy mythology doesn't just build worlds—it shapes minds. It influences how people see death, power, justice, time, even themselves. When you use ChatGPT to create that framework, you're not just adding depth—you're giving your world a voice that speaks from the past into the present.

And now that you've shaped the beliefs, legends, and higher powers of your world, it's time to give your story a solid spine—let's dive into story structure and see how to shape all this worldbuilding into a powerful, gripping narrative.

ChatGPT as Your World-Building Co-Architect

Worldbuilding can feel like both the most exhilarating and overwhelming part of writing fantasy. It's like being handed the blueprints to a blank universe and told, "Build something majestic." Where do you even begin? Should you start with the map, the magic, the religion, the politics, the economy, or the species of talking moss that runs the underground train system? The truth is, you don't need to build everything—you just need to build enough. Enough to make your world feel real. And with ChatGPT as your world-building co-architect, you don't have to do it alone.

Think of ChatGPT as your creative partner who works fast, never runs out of ideas, and doesn't need coffee breaks. When used well, it can help you generate locations, cultures, histories, languages, systems of magic, religions, and creatures in a way that's not only efficient but deeply inspiring. And because ChatGPT is reactive, it lets you build in layers. You can start big, then zoom in, then pivot completely—without ever hitting a wall.

Let's say you start with a rough idea: a kingdom where the sea is sacred, and the people believe their ancestors live in the waves. That alone opens up a cascade of possibilities. You can prompt ChatGPT with something like: *"Describe the customs of a seafaring society that believes the ocean is holy,"* and it might offer traditions for burials at sea, songs sung to summon wind spirits, or laws forbidding the sale of coral. Each of those is a detail you can drop into scenes to make your world feel vivid and coherent.

Now ask about architecture: *"What kind of structures would a sea-worshipping society build?"* You might get ideas about salt-stone temples that glisten at high tide, or homes that collect and channel rainwater as a sacred practice. Then move on to attire: *"What would people wear in a humid coastal kingdom?"* You'll get materials, color palettes, symbols. All of this informs your world without you having to invent every stitch from scratch.

One of the most powerful things about working with ChatGPT is how it lets you explore multiple directions at once. Not sure what kind of government your underwater city should have? Ask for five different options. Want your desert realm to feel different from all the others you've read about? Ask for a list of fresh cultural ideas: *"Give me five unique traditions of a desert tribe that avoids the sun."* You can compare, combine, or reject instantly, refining your world faster than you could brainstorm alone.

ChatGPT is also amazing at *reactive development*. You can say, "In my story, the main city floats in the sky. What challenges would that society face?" and the AI will offer ideas you might not have considered—like weather dangers, caste systems based on elevation, or gravity-defying magic that only the rich can afford. These responses help you uncover the logic of your world, making it stronger and more internally consistent.

When you get stuck, use ChatGPT as your emergency engineer. Can't decide how your hero's homeland should differ from the empire invading it? Ask: *"How might two neighboring fantasy nations differ in culture, economy, and belief?"* or *"Give me contrasts between a nature-based kingdom and a machine-powered empire."* Suddenly, your geopolitical map is forming—and all of it can be written in shorthand until you need more detail.

Another great use of ChatGPT is when you're writing and you realize your world needs a little extra flavor. Maybe your hero stumbles across an old inn. You could just call it "The Resting Mule," or you could ask: *"What would an inn be named in a city that fears night spirits?"* And now you've got *The Last Lantern*, a creaky old place with glowing charms nailed to the beams and a bartender who tells ghost stories to keep the shadows at bay. A five-second prompt has just created setting, mood, and subtext.

If you're designing religions or myths, ChatGPT is an infinite generator of gods, saints, spirits, and creation stories. Ask it to invent a creation myth, and then ask how that myth influences law, art, or education. You'll start to feel how deeply lore can shape a culture. You can say, *"Give me a holiday in a kingdom that celebrates a god of silence,"* and now you have a day each year where no one speaks and violators are cursed with perpetual echo. That kind of detail sticks with readers—and it took you less than a minute to create.

And if you're into languages, you don't have to construct an entire new tongue. You can ask ChatGPT for naming conventions: *"What do names sound like in a society that values harmony and music?"* or *"What might a battle cry sound like in an ancient warrior tribe?"* You'll get vowel patterns, compound names, maybe even invented proverbs. You don't have to build a language—you just need to fake the flavor, and the AI helps you do that fast.

One of the best strategies is to build your world around the *needs of your story*. Don't just worldbuild for the sake of detail. Think in terms of utility. Where does your character go? What do they need to interact with? What do they fear, fight, follow, or flee from? Use ChatGPT to build out only what's necessary, and let the rest stay shadowed in mystery.

You don't need to start with a ten-thousand-year history. You can begin with a single line: *"The moon cracked when the gods fell."* Then ask: *"What are the social, magical, and ecological effects of a cracked moon in a fantasy world?"* The AI will give you enough material for a setting, a religion, a cultural superstition, and probably a plotline or two.

ChatGPT can be the brainstorming partner who's always ready to answer a question, provide a list, expand a sentence, or flip an idea on its head. Use it like a co-architect—your assistant, your muse, your lore-crafter. Build together, tweak together, evolve together. You supply the vision, and ChatGPT helps you sketch the blueprints.

Now that your world is solid beneath your feet—with cities, cultures, creatures, and myths—it's time to turn all that groundwork into motion. Let's shape your fantasy story's structure, so it's not just rich in setting, but also thrilling in pace. Let's talk about plot.

Structuring the Story Before You Write

Fantasy stories have a way of growing like wild vines. One moment, you're describing a glowing stone in a temple ruin, and the next, you're three kingdoms deep into a political rebellion involving a half-dead god and an immortal deer. That's the magic of the genre—its ability to grow and sprawl and surprise. But when you're trying to write a fantasy story in a single day, structure becomes your best friend. Without it, you risk getting lost in your own enchanted forest. With it, you blaze a trail from beginning to end, no matter how strange or spectacular the world may be.

The goal of structuring your story before you write isn't to lock you into a rigid formula—it's to give you a map. And the good news is that fantasy works beautifully with structure. Most epic tales already follow familiar shapes: the hero's journey, the chosen one's rise, the quest narrative, the fall and rise of kingdoms. These shapes are intuitive, and with ChatGPT's help, you can generate and refine them in record time.

The simplest way to begin is to ask yourself: *What kind of story am I telling?* Is it a quest? A rebellion? A mystery? A love story wrapped in prophecy? Once you've got a general sense of the genre or tone within your fantasy framework, you can use ChatGPT to lay the tracks for your plot. For example, you can say: *"Outline a fantasy quest story involving a cursed object and a reluctant hero,"* and you'll immediately get a story skeleton with a beginning, middle, and end. Then you can start plugging in your world, your characters, and your stakes.

One of the most effective story structures, especially for fast writing, is the classic **three-act structure**. You've probably seen this before: Act I introduces the world and the problem, Act II escalates the conflict and deepens the stakes, and Act III brings the resolution and the change. Simple, efficient, and easy to bend to your style. Try this with ChatGPT: *"Give me a three-act fantasy story structure for a story set in a world where magic is illegal."* Now you've got direction—and more importantly, pressure points where your character has to grow or break.

If you want something even simpler, try the **five-scene structure**: the opening, the inciting incident, the midpoint twist, the dark moment, and the resolution. This structure is perfect for short stories, novellas, or one-day projects. It also gives you clear targets to hit, which helps keep you moving. You can ask ChatGPT: *"Give me a five-beat fantasy story structure for a rogue sorcerer trying to resurrect a lost love,"* and you'll get a progression of plot points you can write toward.

Whatever structure you choose, make sure you define **what changes by the end**. That's your compass. Does the protagonist gain power? Lose something precious? Bring peace? Spark war? Change doesn't have to be huge—it just has to matter. Ask: *"What kind of emotional arc fits a story where a young mage leaves their sheltered life and enters a dying magical forest?"* The AI will give you ideas that tie the structure to theme, making your story feel cohesive and intentional.

Use structure to decide **where you need your key beats**. Where does the story open, and why? What kicks it into motion? Where does the tension peak? When does the twist hit? How does the story resolve, and what's left behind? These aren't restrictions—they're creative waypoints. And once you've got them, you'll find that the in-between spaces fill in faster because you're not wandering—you're journeying.

ChatGPT can also help fill those in-between scenes. Let's say you've got your major plot points in place, but you need to bridge them. Ask: *"What should happen between the midpoint reveal and the final battle in a fantasy story involving a cursed bloodline?"* You'll get scenes like alliances, betrayals, training sequences, and revelations—just what you need to keep the momentum.

Structuring also helps with **pacing**, especially in fantasy where it's easy to get bogged down in exposition. If you know when your major events need to happen, you can avoid stuffing too much worldbuilding into the early chapters. You let the reader learn as they go—on the move, through action and dialogue. Try asking: *"How do I pace a fantasy story where the world is unfamiliar to the reader but I don't want to slow down the plot?"* ChatGPT can give you tips like starting in media res, revealing lore through conversation, and saving the deep history for moments of rest.

And structure doesn't mean you can't surprise yourself. In fact, once you've got a clear path, you can play with expectation. Maybe your midpoint twist flips everything. Maybe the villain turns out to be the mentor. Maybe the object of the quest is destroyed just before it's reached. Structure gives you something to subvert. Ask ChatGPT: *"What are some twists I can use in a fantasy story that follows a traditional quest arc?"* The answers can keep your story fresh while still on track.

One more bonus: a solid structure gives you momentum when you're running out of steam. If you hit that midday slump, you don't have to wonder what happens next. You've already set it up. You just have to sit down, tell the next part, and let the characters do what they've been built to do. Structure is your safety net when inspiration fades—and ChatGPT is the co-writer who keeps pushing you forward.

So before you start the actual drafting, take an hour with your map. Use your prompts. Nail down the shape of your story. It doesn't need to be detailed. Just clear. Beginning, middle, end. Conflict, twist, change. If you know where you're going, the writing flows like magic.

Three Acts and a Portal: Plotting Your Fantasy Adventure

Every good fantasy story has that moment—the point of no return—when the hero steps through the portal, crosses the threshold, or makes the choice that alters everything. It could be literal, like stepping into a new realm, or symbolic, like defying an ancient law. Either way, that moment is usually nestled right in the transition between the first and second act. And that's where plotting a fantasy adventure using the classic three-act structure becomes more than just a tool—it becomes your story's spine.

Let's start at the top. The **three-act structure** is a timeless, flexible blueprint for storytelling. In fantasy, it's especially useful because you're often working with sprawling ideas, massive worldbuilding, and high-stakes character arcs. A three-act structure keeps all that imaginative chaos in check, making sure your story moves instead of meanders.

Act I is all about establishing your world and introducing your protagonist. This is the "before" picture—the quiet before the storm. But in fantasy, you've got a little more work to do. You're not just introducing a hero; you're introducing a *world* with its own rules, cultures, and creatures. That doesn't mean frontloading exposition. It means choosing smart ways to show what's normal *right now* so that when everything changes, the reader feels the shift.

Use ChatGPT to help you sketch this setup fast. Ask something like: *"Give me Act I story beats for a reluctant hero living in a cursed village,"* or *"Describe the daily life of a stable boy in a kingdom where dragons are outlawed."* This isn't just backstory—it's a way to ground the reader in something they can emotionally connect with. The key is contrast: whatever your world looks like at the beginning, it won't stay that way for long.

Then comes the **Inciting Incident**—the spark that sets the journey in motion. A letter arrives. A murder is witnessed. A relic is stolen. A monster breaches the walls. You can prompt ChatGPT with: *"What's a compelling inciting incident for a story about a hidden magical bloodline?"* This is the moment your story breaks open. Everything that follows is a reaction to it.

Which brings us to the end of Act I: the **Portal Moment**. This can be literal, like walking into another dimension, or metaphorical, like swearing an oath or breaking a rule that can't be undone. The hero doesn't always go willingly. Sometimes they're dragged through the portal kicking and screaming. Other times, they leap in, heart pounding, with no plan at all. The important thing is that once it happens, they can't go back.

Ask ChatGPT to help dramatize this threshold: *"What might a portal look like in a world built from dreams?"* or *"Describe the emotional stakes of a character who chooses exile over silence."* This moment should feel huge—because it is. It's the turn into Act II, where the real fun begins.

Act II is the heart of your story, and in fantasy, it's often the biggest act. This is where you explore the unknown, deepen relationships, test your protagonist, and twist the plot. The hero learns new rules, meets allies and enemies, and starts to change. Use prompts like: *"What kind of trials would a magical warrior face while traveling through a kingdom ruled by illusions?"* or *"Give me ways to build tension between a chosen hero and a secretive guide."*

You'll want to include a **midpoint twist**—something that turns the story in a new direction. The villain isn't who they seemed. The prophecy was misread. The magical relic is a trap. Midpoints don't just shock the reader—they raise the stakes. Ask ChatGPT: *"What's a midpoint reveal in a story where the hero thinks they're on the right side of history?"* Suddenly, your world feels layered and your plot kicks into high gear.

The second half of Act II usually brings your hero to their **lowest point**. Betrayal. Defeat. Capture. Loss. This is the moment they doubt everything—including themselves. Their powers fail. Their allies scatter. Their hope fades. This is the dark cave, the dungeon, the curse that nearly breaks them. Prompt: *"Describe a magical trial that forces the hero to confront their deepest fear,"* or *"Create a scene where the protagonist learns a devastating truth about their origin."*

Then, just when it seems the hero might give up, something shifts. They find new resolve. An old friend returns. A hidden truth is revealed. They emerge changed. Ready.

And that brings us to **Act III**, the final movement. This is where everything the hero has learned, suffered, and sacrificed comes to a head. They return to the place of conflict—physically or spiritually—with clarity and power. The final act isn't just about beating the bad guy; it's about fulfilling the arc. If your story began with a selfish loner, the finale should show them risking everything for someone else. If it began with someone powerless, they should now stand tall—still flawed, but transformed.

The climax should reflect both outer conflict and inner growth. Ask ChatGPT: *"What does a final battle look like between a hero who has mastered empathy and a villain who thrives on control?"* or *"Describe an ending where the protagonist defeats the villain but chooses mercy over vengeance."* You'll discover how to weave theme into action, making the conclusion not just thrilling, but meaningful.

The resolution, or **denouement**, ties it all together. A return home. A kingdom rebuilt. A new journey beginning. Not every question needs an answer, but the emotional journey must feel complete. You can ask: *"How might a fantasy story end with both hope and sorrow?"* or *"Describe a peaceful ending that still leaves room for a sequel."*

Using the three-act structure as a foundation, and letting ChatGPT help you sketch scenes, spark twists, and fill gaps, you can plot a fantasy adventure that feels tight, complete, and emotionally satisfying—even if it was written in a day.

The Prophecy Hook: Creating Urgency from Page One

There's something irresistibly powerful about a prophecy. It adds instant tension, mystery, and weight to a fantasy story. From the very first page, it whispers, *this was always meant to happen... or was it?* Prophecies suggest fate, but they also suggest defiance. They create a sense that the world is bigger than what's on the page—that something ancient and unseen is pulling the strings, and the characters are just beginning to understand how tangled the threads really are. That's why the prophecy hook is one of the sharpest tools you can use to create urgency from the start of your fantasy adventure.

But not all prophecies are created equal. The most effective ones don't just sound poetic—they ripple through the story. They force choices, stir conflict, and shadow every scene with uncertainty. And with ChatGPT, you can spin a prophecy from thin air in seconds, then twist it into something memorable, dangerous, and alive.

Start with the basics. Ask ChatGPT: *"Create a prophecy that foretells the rise of a hero from a forgotten bloodline,"* or *"Write a vague, ominous prophecy that sounds like it could refer to either the hero or the villain."* You'll get poetic riddles, ancient inscriptions, or chilling rhymes carved into obsidian stones. These aren't just cool flavor—they give you a spine to build your plot around. From the very first page, the reader knows something big is coming.

What makes a prophecy hook work is its **immediacy**. It's not just about what might happen someday—it's about something that has already begun. Your protagonist doesn't need to *understand* the prophecy yet. Maybe they overhear it, maybe someone reads it to them, maybe they stumble across it half-erased on a tomb wall. The important thing is that the moment it's mentioned, the reader feels the fuse has been lit.

And the best part? You don't have to explain it right away. In fact, the vaguer and more open to interpretation it is, the more room you have to twist it later. Fantasy thrives on prophecies that seem to mean one thing and turn out to mean something else. Try asking ChatGPT: *"Give me a prophecy that misleads the characters until the final act,"* or *"Write a prophecy that sounds hopeful but hides a tragic outcome."* This kind of misdirection gives you built-in plot twists without needing to invent new complications mid-story.

Another powerful angle is **personal prophecy**—when the message isn't about the world, but about the character. The chosen one, the betrayer, the last heir, the unknowing key to an ancient lock. These roles immediately raise the stakes. Your character isn't just surviving—they're a piece in an ancient puzzle. Ask ChatGPT: *"Create a prophecy tied to a character born with a scar shaped like a crescent moon,"* or *"What might a dying seer whisper to a child destined to shatter kingdoms?"* These moments hit hard, and they stick.

But be careful with the "chosen one" cliché. You can breathe new life into it by flipping the expectation. Maybe the prophecy is fake. Maybe it was meant for someone else. Maybe your protagonist was misidentified. Try prompts like: *"Write a prophecy that everyone believes—but it was planted as a political tool,"* or *"Create a prophecy that has been mistranslated for centuries."* Now your hero isn't just trying to fulfill destiny—they're questioning it. Fighting it. Maybe even rewriting it.

You can also connect the prophecy directly to **conflict**. If your villain knows the prophecy too, they might try to stop it—or force it. If the prophecy says one shall rise and one shall fall, who decides which is which? You can ask ChatGPT to explore both sides: *"What might a villain do to prevent a prophecy from coming true?"* or *"How would a kingdom react if they feared a child was the one from a dark prophecy?"* This takes the prophecy from background detail to central engine.

In worldbuilding terms, prophecy also adds **history and culture**. Maybe there's an entire religious order devoted to interpreting ancient signs. Maybe the stars are charted every night to look for omens. Maybe the last person named in a prophecy brought ruin to the world—and now your hero is suspected of the same. Ask: *"How would a fantasy society that believes in prophecy treat those marked by fate?"* or *"What might a heretical cult believe about an ancient prediction?"* The answer shapes your world with instant mythology.

Prophecies can also fuel relationships. Maybe a character is torn between friendship and fate. Maybe they fall in love with someone they're destined to betray. Maybe they hide a piece of the prophecy out of fear. These dynamics bring emotional depth to a story that could otherwise just be a string of battles and quests. Use prompts like: *"Create romantic tension between two characters destined to destroy each other,"* or *"Describe the guilt of a character who hides a prophecy from the group."*

And remember—the prophecy doesn't have to be true. It just has to *matter*. If the characters believe it, the prophecy shapes their decisions, whether or not it ever comes to pass. That's where the real tension lies. You can use ChatGPT to test the consequences: *"What happens if a character acts out of fear of a prophecy and causes the very thing they tried to stop?"* or *"How could a false prophecy become self-fulfilling?"* These story paths are rich with irony, tragedy, and drama.

By starting your story with a prophecy—or even hinting at one—you create a sense of momentum from the first paragraph. It doesn't just say *things will happen.* It says *things are meant to happen.* And that pulls the reader forward, always wondering, *Is this it? Is this the moment it begins—or the one it ends?*

So write your prophecy. Etch it into a temple wall. Whisper it in a dying breath. Paint it in stars. Then let it haunt your characters. Let it guide them, torment them, or mislead them. Because once a prophecy enters the story, there's no going back.

The Chosen One and Other Classic Tropes You Can Use or Twist

Fantasy thrives on tropes. The chosen one. The ancient evil. The wise old mentor. The prophecy. The magical sword. These building blocks are familiar for a reason—they've worked for centuries. Readers love them not because they're new, but because they feel like home. The trick is not to avoid tropes, but to *own* them. Use them with purpose. Twist them with flair. Subvert them when it makes the story better. And when you're writing a fantasy story in a single day, working with tropes is one of the fastest ways to create a satisfying, cohesive story. With ChatGPT helping along the way, you can explore, remix, and reinvent these classics on the fly.

Let's start with the big one: **the Chosen One**. It's the trope that refuses to die—because when it's done well, it taps into something deep and universal. The idea that someone seemingly ordinary has an extraordinary destiny. It's empowering. It's mythic. But it can also be predictable if you don't give it your own spin.

If you want to use the Chosen One trope straight up, you can keep it fresh by focusing on what *makes* the person chosen. Is it a birthmark? A dream? A bloodline? A fluke? Try a prompt like: *"Create a unique reason a character is considered the Chosen One in a magical society."* Maybe the character survived a storm that should've killed them. Maybe they were born during an eclipse that silenced magic. You want something specific and story-relevant—not just "they're special because they are."

But what if you twist it?

Ask: *"What if the Chosen One doesn't want to be chosen?"* or *"What if the prophecy was misinterpreted and the real Chosen One is the antagonist?"* These versions build tension and complexity. Your hero might spend the story trying to escape their fate, only to find that they're the only one who can stop what's coming. Or maybe they find out someone else was better suited, but it's too late to switch roles.

Another fun twist: *What if everyone believes they're the Chosen One?* You could have multiple characters, all convinced the prophecy points to them, and the tension comes from their clashing egos, interpretations, and actions. Ask ChatGPT: *"Describe a scenario where three characters each believe they're the chosen saviour."* Instant conflict—and room for drama, betrayal, and surprise.

Once you've played with the Chosen One, look at the other tropes in your fantasy toolbox. There's the **wise mentor**, for instance. Usually old, cryptic, and doomed to die right before the hero's big test. You can use this classic setup—or flip it. What if the mentor is younger than the hero? What if they're unreliable or selfish? What if they're still learning, too? Ask ChatGPT: *"Give me five unconventional fantasy mentor archetypes,"* and you'll get ideas like a drunk oracle, a ghostly bard, or a talking animal who resents being bound to the hero.

Then there's the **ancient evil**—the dark force sealed long ago, now stirring again. Great for raising stakes and tying your story into a larger history. But again, you can twist it. Maybe the "evil" was misrepresented in old records. Maybe it's not a person but a concept, like greed or despair, given shape by the people's fear. Try: *"Describe an ancient evil that was created unintentionally by a society's obsession with purity,"* or *"What if the ancient evil is actually trying to save the world from a greater threat?"* This kind of depth gives your villain real weight.

Don't forget the **magical weapon** trope—your Excaliburs, your enchanted daggers, your staves carved from the bones of gods. These objects are fun because they're visual, symbolic, and often tied to the character arc. But you can easily spin the idea by asking: *"Create a magical weapon that harms the user as much as the enemy,"* or *"What kind of enchanted item would a pacifist carry into battle?"* ChatGPT can help you brainstorm gear that does more than glow—it tells a story.

Other tropes worth using or twisting:

- **The Secret Royalty**: The orphan hero turns out to be heir to the throne. Classic. But what if they *reject* the crown? What if they're hunted for it? Or what if the throne no longer exists?
- **The Fellowship or Quest Team**: A group of misfits joins forces. But maybe they don't trust each other. Maybe one is a spy. Maybe the quest is a lie. Ask: *"Design a quest team where each member has a hidden agenda."*
- **The Prophecy** (which we already covered): Consider a story where the prophecy doesn't come true—or worse, where it does, and it's a tragedy.
- **The Magical School**: Hogwarts started the trend, but you can push it further. Maybe magic is taught underground. Maybe students steal their lessons from other worlds. Or maybe there's no teaching—just survival.

Each of these tropes has power because readers *know* them. That recognition creates a shortcut to meaning. But the real magic happens when you use that recognition to surprise them.

Let's say you start with a prompt like: *"Outline a story where the Chosen One is actually the villain and doesn't know it yet."* You now have a full arc of irony, tragedy, and suspense. Or maybe you try: *"Create a story where the mentor is trying to prevent the hero from fulfilling the prophecy."* That one twist reframes every interaction and keeps the reader guessing.

You can even mash up tropes. What happens when a secret royal is also the villain? When the ancient evil is a misunderstood child? When the magical weapon chooses someone completely unworthy? Ask for combos like: *"Mix the tropes of the reluctant hero and the villainous prophecy to create a story outline."* ChatGPT will hand you fresh angles that blend familiar ideas in ways that feel original.

The key isn't avoiding tropes—it's using them with intention. Know what each one does for your story. Know how to play it straight, how to turn it on its head, and when to let it do both at the same time. Tropes are tools, and in the right hands, they build unforgettable tales.

Now that we've explored how tropes can shape your plot, let's shift to the deep internal side of storytelling. In the next chapter, we'll explore **why fantasy needs stakes—and how to raise them.**

Why Fantasy Needs Stakes: Creating Meaningful Conflict

Fantasy, with all its magic and wonder, often gives the illusion that anything is possible. Cast a spell, summon a beast, invoke an ancient god, or rewrite destiny with a drop of blood and a whisper. It's intoxicating—and dangerously easy to slip into writing where problems vanish with a wand wave or where tension fizzles because everything feels too safe, too easy, too distant. That's where **stakes** come in. If fantasy is the stage, then stakes are the fire that burns beneath it. They give your story weight. They make your characters' choices matter. Without them, even the most imaginative world falls flat.

Stakes are what your character stands to **lose**. And not just personally, but emotionally, morally, spiritually, or even cosmically. They create urgency. They push your characters forward when everything in them screams to stop. The higher the stakes—or the more personal and specific—the more readers invest. So how do you build them? And how do you keep them sharp in a story that might include dragons, dream-walkers, or talking wolves made of starlight?

Start with the **character**. What does your protagonist care about more than anything? A sibling. A village. Their identity. Their freedom. Their past. It doesn't have to be world-shattering—but it has to be theirs. Ask ChatGPT: *"What's a deeply personal stake for a hero who's afraid of becoming their father?"* or *"Give me emotional stakes for a character tasked with protecting a child they don't believe in."* These stakes build tension that resonates beyond just plot mechanics—they speak to who your character is becoming.

Then scale those personal stakes outward. What happens if they fail? Does the village burn? Does magic disappear? Does a sealed evil wake beneath the world? This is where you can layer your story with **external stakes**—things that affect the world, the people, or the very fabric of the realm. You can prompt ChatGPT: *"Describe world-ending consequences for a character who fails to complete a magical ritual,"* or *"What happens if the hero fails to unite the feuding kingdoms?"* External stakes add scope, but they're most powerful when they grow out of internal ones.

Conflict emerges when stakes **collide**. Maybe the hero must choose between saving someone they love and saving the world. Maybe using magic to stop the villain also destroys the thing they swore to protect. These moments are gold—they force decisions. Ask ChatGPT: *"Create a moral dilemma for a hero who is torn between loyalty to their people and a forbidden love,"* or *"What's a tragic consequence of defeating the villain too soon?"* Conflict that matters always comes back to what's truly at risk.

Stakes don't have to be epic in size—they just need to be **urgent and irreversible**. A magical disease with no cure. A curse that worsens every time a character lies. A pact with a spirit that steals a memory each time a spell is cast. These are high-stakes choices packed into every moment. Try prompts like: *"What's a magical cost that grows more dangerous with each use?"* or *"Describe an enchanted bond that grows stronger the more it's resisted."* These kinds of stakes keep tension high with every page.

In fantasy, it's tempting to think that magic solves everything. But what if it makes things worse? That's where the stakes really sing. Maybe magic saves a friend—but leaves the caster marked, hunted, or hollow. Maybe the hero succeeds in winning the war but unleashes a forgotten god in the process. These ripple effects matter. Use ChatGPT to generate cause-and-effect sequences: *"What happens if a sorcerer uses forbidden blood magic to stop a battle?"* or *"Give me unexpected consequences for reviving a fallen ally."*

Stakes also affect **theme**. A story about power should make your character risk losing control. A story about identity should force them to sacrifice who they thought they were. Ask: *"What's at stake in a story about a hero questioning their* *destiny?"* or *"Describe what a character might lose in a story about forbidden knowledge."* When stakes align with your theme, the entire story feels more cohesive.

You can also raise the stakes throughout your story to keep things escalating. What starts as a personal quest becomes political, then magical, then metaphysical. Maybe the hero just wants to escape a cursed forest—but learns that doing so will unleash a sleeping monster into the world. Try asking ChatGPT: *"How can I raise the stakes from personal survival to world-threatening in a short fantasy story?"* This lets you build tension in waves, drawing the reader deeper with each escalation.

And don't forget to give **every character** their own stakes. Even your villain should have something to lose—pride, power, peace, or even love. Secondary characters might have goals that clash with the protagonist's. These side-stakes create layered conflict. Ask: *"What's at stake for a reluctant ally who fears the hero's success?"* or *"Describe a villain who believes destroying the world is an act of mercy."* When everyone is risking something, every conversation can spark with tension.

One final trick: make the reader believe something *won't* happen—and then let it happen. Kill the mentor. Burn the village. Break the sword. Let the magic run out. If you've built real stakes, these moments will hit hard, because readers believed the characters could avoid them. That emotional whiplash keeps fantasy stories from feeling safe or predictable.

So don't let your world's beauty dull the danger. Give your characters something to fight for, something to fear losing, something that will change them forever if it slips away. That's what turns magic into meaning, and wonder into weight.

Now that your characters are risking everything, it's time to balance the high drama with the finer strokes of characterization. Let's talk about **side characters**—those allies, rivals, and oddballs who bring depth, heart, and friction to the fantasy journey.

Side Characters Who Steal the Show

Every fantasy story has a main character—the chosen one, the exiled prince, the cursed mage—but often, it's the side characters who truly steal the show. You know the ones. The rogue with too many secrets. The talking animal with better one-liners than the hero. The grizzled mercenary who's done with everything but can't stop helping. Side characters bring heart, flavor, and surprise to a story. They're the ones readers fall in love with, quote endlessly, and sometimes wish had their own spin-off series. And when you're writing a fantasy story in a single day, well-drawn side characters can elevate your world, deepen your plot, and keep things moving when your hero starts to stall.

The first thing to understand is that a great side character is never just a support beam. They're not there to be furniture. They're not there to agree with the hero, and they're definitely not there just to die for motivation. The best ones have lives of their own. Histories. Dreams. Agendas. Even if the reader doesn't see all of it, they'll *feel* that these characters exist beyond the frame.

Start with role. Ask yourself: what kind of energy does this story need? If your hero is serious and solemn, maybe they need a sarcastic sidekick. If they're reckless, they might need a cautious advisor. If they're an outsider, they need someone who knows the lay of the land. Use ChatGPT to brainstorm personalities that create contrast: *"Give me a list of fantasy side characters who challenge the protagonist's worldview,"* or *"Invent a companion who secretly resents the hero."* That tension makes every scene richer.

Then layer in backstory. It doesn't have to be long—just enough to suggest depth. Maybe the warrior refuses to touch magic because their sibling vanished into a spell gone wrong. Maybe the innkeeper with a missing arm used to be a battle mage. Ask ChatGPT: *"Give me a one-line tragic backstory for a charming thief,"* or *"Describe the secret history of a side character who once betrayed a kingdom."* These little details make characters unforgettable.

A strong side character also brings unique skills or knowledge to the table. The story's progress often depends on them, even if the spotlight stays on the main hero. Maybe they speak a forgotten language. Maybe they know the secret entrance to the ancient vault. Or maybe they're the only one who can see the ghosts haunting the road ahead. Try a prompt like: *"Invent a fantasy sidekick with a magical ability that's both useful and dangerous,"* or *"What kind of guide would survive in a city built atop a sleeping dragon?"*

The best side characters also *grow*. They don't have to have a full arc, but they shouldn't stay flat either. Maybe the bitter warrior learns to hope again. Maybe the coward finds courage in the final act. Maybe the comic relief character drops the joke long enough to say something that breaks your heart. Ask: *"Give me an emotional moment for a side character who masks their grief with humor,"* or *"Describe how a side character might grow after failing the protagonist."* These beats add emotional weight to your story.

Side characters can also serve as mirrors to the protagonist. They reflect different paths, different choices. Maybe they show what the hero could become—or what they might've been. The noble knight who gave into vengeance. The villain's apprentice who walked away. The sibling who chose duty over desire. Use ChatGPT to help you find these parallels: *"Create a side character whose life reflects what the hero could become if they choose fear over courage."*

You can also give side characters their own goals—goals that don't align with the hero's. That's when scenes get spicy. Maybe your ally is helping you get to the cursed city because they want to steal the relic for themselves. Maybe your healer has a deal with the enemy to protect their homeland. These kinds of internal conflicts make every conversation more loaded. Ask: *"Describe a side character whose secret agenda clashes with the hero's mission."* The more personal the stakes, the more unpredictable the interactions.

And yes—some side characters *are* there to die. But make sure their death means something. It should change the hero. Reveal something new. Shift the direction of the story. Don't fridge them. Make their loss a turning point, not a throwaway shock. If you need to kill someone off, ask ChatGPT: *"How can the death of a side character transform the protagonist's choices?"* That way, it's not just loss—it's momentum.

Side characters also let you show off the world. Through them, you can explore different cultures, social roles, types of magic, or historical events without long-winded exposition. A pirate queen tells you about maritime law. A talking crow reveals the legends of the old gods. A cursed knight teaches you the etiquette of war among the undead. Ask: *"Create a side character who can deliver lore through dialogue without sounding like exposition,"* and let them carry that worldbuilding for you.

And don't underestimate comic relief. A funny, awkward, or chaotic character can keep the tone from getting too heavy. But even here, depth matters. The fool often sees the truth before anyone else. The coward sometimes makes the bravest call. Try: *"Give me a comedic fantasy sidekick with hidden wisdom,"* or *"What might a jester character reveal about the truth behind the king's madness?"* Humor and tragedy often walk hand in hand in the best fantasy tales.

Ultimately, great side characters feel like they *could* be the hero of their own story. And that's the trick. Whether they're with your protagonist for five pages or fifty, they should leave an impression. They should complicate the story, not just help move it along. They should be unpredictable, flawed, memorable.

So let ChatGPT help you design them quickly—but fill them with life as you write. Let them improvise, surprise, argue, save, betray, laugh, and bleed. Let them matter.

Next, we'll step into the sacred halls of the fantasy archetype—the **mentor**. Let's explore how to craft a guide figure who doesn't just dump wisdom and vanish, but shapes the story with presence, power, and maybe even a few secrets of their own.

The Mentor, the Trickster, and the Rival

If your protagonist is the soul of your fantasy story, then the supporting archetypes—especially the mentor, the trickster, and the rival—are the forces that test, shape, and sharpen that soul. Each of these characters brings tension and depth to the narrative in their own way. They challenge the hero from different angles: one teaches, one disrupts, one competes. Used well, they don't just support the plot—they fuel it. And when you're writing fast, like crafting a story in a single day, having strong archetypal figures in place helps you create impact quickly. Even better? With ChatGPT, you can build, twist, and repurpose these archetypes with ease.

Let's start with the **Mentor**—the classic wise guide. They usually appear early in the story, offering knowledge, prophecy, a sword, or a push out the door. Think Gandalf, Dumbledore, or Obi-Wan. But don't settle for the default old wizard in a cloak unless that's exactly what your story needs. Ask yourself: *What kind of mentor does my protagonist actually need?* Not just someone who knows more, but someone who reflects the hero's flaws, fears, or future.

Use ChatGPT to brainstorm unique mentor types: *"Give me five unconventional fantasy mentor characters,"* or *"Create a mentor who challenges the hero's morality instead of confirming it."* You might end up with a bitter ex-hero who failed their own quest. A mute librarian who communicates through enchanted books. A villain-turned-guide trying to redeem themselves. The best mentors don't just advise—they provoke. They force the hero to grow. They make things harder, not easier.

And here's a classic twist: the **mentor doesn't stay**. They die, vanish, betray, or simply step aside. It's a rite of passage. The story shifts when the hero can no longer lean on them. Ask ChatGPT: *"How can a mentor's departure force the protagonist to grow?"* or *"Give me a plot twist where the mentor was hiding the truth all along."* These are more than plot devices—they're turning points in your character arc.

Now let's talk about the **Trickster**—chaotic, unpredictable, and wildly fun to write. This character lives in the cracks of the world. They aren't bound by tradition or morality. They might lie, laugh, disappear mid-scene, or leave riddles instead of help. But often, they're the only one telling the truth.

The trickster tests the hero, not by fighting them, but by *confusing* them. They blur the lines between friend and foe. Maybe they guide the hero to safety—and then pickpocket them. Maybe they sabotage the plan—but only to save lives in the long run. Ask ChatGPT: *"Create a fantasy trickster who manipulates events behind the scenes,"* or *"Describe a character who uses humor to expose painful truths."*

You can use the trickster to inject energy into your scenes, to deliver exposition in a playful way, or to add twists where the plot needs a jolt. And don't underestimate their heart. Some tricksters are broken people who laugh to avoid crying. Some are former heroes themselves, choosing chaos because they've lost faith in order. You can ask: *"What motivates a trickster who keeps helping people but claims they don't care?"*

Then there's the **Rival**—the one who pushes the protagonist by standing in their way, not out of malice, but because they have their own path to follow. They might be competing for the same relic, love interest, title, or destiny. They might even be better than the hero—stronger, smarter, more respected. That's what makes the rivalry burn. It's not hatred—it's friction. The rival forces the hero to evolve.

A great rival is more than an obstacle—they're a shadow self. What your hero *could* become under different circumstances. You can prompt ChatGPT: *"Give me a fantasy rival who mirrors the hero's worst fear,"* or *"Describe a rival who believes they're the real chosen one."* When you write them well, every scene between the hero and the rival feels electric.

You can also make the rival an **ally in disguise**. Maybe they start off as enemies but end up fighting back-to-back. Maybe their respect grows over time. Or maybe the opposite happens—trust turns to betrayal. Ask ChatGPT: *"What are some turning points in a rivalry that becomes a friendship—or a tragedy?"* These arcs are full of emotion and momentum.

Together, the mentor, trickster, and rival form a triangle of tension around the hero. One guides, one confuses, one competes. They each reflect different parts of your protagonist's identity—and push them in different directions. The mentor asks, *Who will you become?* The trickster asks, *What do you really believe?* The rival asks, *Are you strong enough to win?*

You don't need all three. But if you use them, make them count. Give them presence. Let them speak, act, and break things. Let them matter. Ask ChatGPT to help sketch arcs for each one: *"Give me a character arc for a rival who becomes a martyr,"* or *"Describe a mentor who turns antagonist because the hero ignores their teaching."*

And don't forget—these roles can overlap. The rival can become a mentor. The trickster can betray the hero and then return at the final hour. The mentor might turn out to have been the rival all along. Archetypes aren't boxes—they're starting points. What matters is how your characters shift within and beyond them.

So build these characters not as accessories, but as engines of change. Let them move through the story with fire in their veins and secrets in their pockets.

Next, we'll shift to shaping your scenes: how to craft powerful moments of conflict, discovery, or connection—one scene at a time—with ChatGPT helping you build your narrative step by step.

Writing a Strong Opening Scene with AI's Help

The opening scene of your fantasy story is everything. It's the gateway into your world, the spark that lights your plot, and the first thread that ties the reader to your protagonist. Whether you're crafting a high fantasy epic or a cozy magical adventure, those first few pages set the tone, promise the stakes, and ask the reader to trust you enough to keep going. And when you're writing a story in a single day, the opening scene isn't just important—it's your launchpad. You need it to fire on all cylinders. This is where ChatGPT becomes your co-pilot, helping you build the right atmosphere, pick the right moment, and choose the best words to draw readers in fast.

So where do you start?

The best opening scenes usually do a few things at once: they establish setting, introduce the protagonist, suggest conflict, and hook the reader with a bit of mystery or tension. That's a lot to juggle in one scene, which is why using AI to organize or draft these layers can save you serious time.

Begin with the big picture: **what kind of opening moment fits your story?** Is it quiet and eerie? Loud and chaotic? Emotional? Funny? Ask ChatGPT: *"Give me five types of fantasy opening scenes for a story about a cursed royal heir,"* or *"Suggest an atmospheric opening scene for a dark forest fantasy tale."* You'll get options ranging from battlefields to moonlit markets to prison cells that speak in riddles.

Once you know the general vibe, you can narrow in on what *needs* to happen in this scene. Maybe you need to show that your world is dangerous. Maybe your hero needs to witness something strange. Maybe they need to make a choice that pushes them down a new path. Ask: *"What's a strong inciting incident to begin a fantasy story about forbidden magic?"* or *"Describe a scene where the protagonist discovers their powers in a public place."*

With those building blocks in place, you can start crafting actual prose. If you're staring at a blank page, try prompting ChatGPT with a line like: *"Write the first paragraph of a fantasy story where a village elder sacrifices a secret to keep the forest spirits quiet."* What you get might not be your final draft, but it gives you tone, momentum, and language to build from. You can edit it, expand it, or rewrite it completely—but you're no longer facing an empty screen.

A great trick is to open *mid-action*—but not necessarily mid-battle. Action just means movement. It could be your hero sneaking into a sacred hall. Running from a debt collector. Stealing bread from a market stall while guards march by. Opening mid-action gives readers a feeling that the story has already begun—and they've arrived just in time. Ask: *"Give me an opening scene where a thief accidentally steals a cursed object,"* or *"Describe a tense moment that introduces a fantasy hero in hiding."*

And don't underestimate the power of **dialogue** in the first scene. It can establish voice, introduce relationships, and hint at deeper story threads. Try asking ChatGPT: *"Write a short exchange between a mentor and their student just before a forbidden ritual,"* or *"Create a dialogue that hints at a prophecy without saying it outright."* You'll instantly add motion and personality to your scene.

Opening scenes are also your first chance to **ground the world**. What do people wear? What does the air smell like? What strange customs are happening in the background? You don't need pages of description—just a few key details to spark the reader's imagination. Use ChatGPT to help generate sensory language: *"Describe a fantasy marketplace during a magical eclipse,"* or *"Give me visual details for a forest where time runs backward."* These descriptions give your world texture and life.

A strong opening also leaves **a question hanging**. Not necessarily a literal question, but something that makes the reader lean in. Why was the child alone in the ruins? Why is everyone afraid of the sky tonight? Why did the hero flinch at the sight of a crown? Try asking ChatGPT: *"Write a fantasy opening scene that ends with an eerie unanswered question,"* or *"Create a mysterious moment that hints at a magical threat without revealing it."*

You can also use the AI to create **alternatives**. If you're not sure whether to open with a prophecy, a battle, or a quiet domestic moment that gets shattered, ask: *"Give me three possible opening scenes for a fantasy story about a girl who unknowingly carries a piece of a dead god."* You'll get different tones and angles, and you can quickly test which one feels right for your story.

Even if you already know what your first scene will be, ChatGPT can help you refine it. Ask it to rewrite your scene with more tension, more dialogue, or more sensory detail. You can prompt: *"Enhance this scene to build more suspense,"* or *"Rephrase this so the character's voice feels more distinct."* The AI becomes your editor, punching up your prose in real-time.

And most importantly, don't get stuck. The opening scene doesn't have to be perfect. It just has to *begin*. With a clear structure, a compelling tone, and a bit of AI help, you can start strong—and then let the story carry you from there.

Dialogue That Feels Real in Unreal Worlds

Fantasy is filled with dragons, spells, ancient prophecies, and glowing swords—but none of it works if the characters sound like they're reading off a script. No matter how strange the setting, readers connect with stories through people—and people speak. That means dialogue is one of your most powerful tools for making a fantasy world feel real. It gives your characters soul, shapes their relationships, reveals their secrets, and moves the story forward. And when you're writing a fantasy story in a single day, strong dialogue keeps the momentum alive and your characters vivid from scene one. Luckily, ChatGPT is great at helping you generate, fine-tune, and experiment with dialogue that works in any kind of world.

The first rule? **Even in fantasy, people should still sound like people.** They might use different words, have odd turns of phrase, or reference ancient events, but their emotions should be recognizable. Fear still sounds like fear. Joy still bubbles. Anger still cuts. If your dialogue is too stiff, too formal, or too loaded with exposition, it risks losing the reader—even if it's "realistic" for your world.

Start with tone. Ask ChatGPT: *"Give me dialogue between a nervous apprentice and a stoic mentor right before a forbidden spell is cast."* You'll get something with tension, power dynamics, and probably a few hints of backstory. Then you can rewrite or reshape it to match your characters exactly. The goal isn't perfection—it's to get the emotional truth across.

Next, make sure your characters speak **in their own voices**. A soldier and a scholar shouldn't sound the same. A street thief's sentences will be clipped, informal, maybe a bit clever. A royal diplomat might speak in long, smooth patterns with carefully chosen words. Ask ChatGPT: *"Write the same sentence in the voices of a thief, a noble, and a young mage,"* and you'll see how tone and background shape word choice.

You can also use dialogue to **reveal the world organically**. Instead of explaining that a magical tax has been imposed on every spell-caster, have two characters argue about it. "I'm not paying a copper for casting light in my own house!" one might shout, while the other warns, "That's how they caught Brenner—one flicker and the watch was at his door." Now the reader knows the rule, the consequence, and the tone of the world—all through voice.

Ask ChatGPT: *"Create a dialogue between two fantasy characters discussing a new law banning flight spells,"* and watch how it turns a piece of worldbuilding into a scene with stakes and personality.

Tension is your friend. Not every line needs to be a full-blown argument, but friction keeps dialogue interesting. Two characters want the same thing for different reasons. One knows a secret the other doesn't. One's joking to cover up fear. Ask for these dynamics directly: *"Write a conversation where one character is hiding a lie and the other is trying to figure it out."*

Dialogue is also where you can play with **humor**, especially if your story leans dark. A sarcastic sidekick or a jaded mercenary can provide levity that balances out the grim prophecies and violent quests. Ask ChatGPT: *"Give me a funny exchange between a talking horse and the hero who's trying to ride it into battle,"* or *"Write dry banter between two old mages stuck in a collapsing library."* A little wit can make even the weirdest worlds feel grounded.

And don't be afraid to **cut and tighten**. When using ChatGPT to draft dialogue, you might get more than you need. That's okay. You can pare it down. One strong line can say more than five average ones. If a character says, "You lied to me," that's fine. But if they say, "Funny how silence can be louder than any truth," now it's memorable. Ask the AI to help sharpen your lines: *"Rewrite this sentence to sound more threatening,"* or *"Make this line more poetic."*

When writing fantasy dialogue, also think about **cultural flavor**. People from different lands or races might have specific sayings or speech rhythms. A character from a desert kingdom might speak in metaphors about wind, sand, and thirst. An elf who lives centuries might talk slowly and in circles. You can use prompts like: *"Create idioms for a mountain-dwelling culture that worships the sky,"* and then drop those phrases into your dialogue to build immersion.

But above all—**don't let dialogue stall the story**. Every conversation should reveal something, move something, or deepen something. If two characters talk just to explain lore, the scene will drag. If they argue, joke, confess, or threaten each other—now you've got momentum. You can always refine the wording later, but get the core tension right first.

And if you need variety fast, ChatGPT can create different styles on demand: *"Give me formal dialogue between two queens negotiating a ceasefire,"* or *"Write awkward first-time banter between a bard and a grumpy innkeeper."* Use these samples as scaffolding, then revise to match your story's unique voice.

So as you bring your world to life, remember this: glowing swords and shadow beasts are fun, but it's the way your characters talk to each other that will stick in readers' minds. Their voices—sarcastic, scared, furious, hopeful—are what make fantasy *feel* real.

Next, let's look at how to write **scene transitions and keep the story flowing**, even when you're rushing from a dragon's lair to a haunted riverbank to a crumbling tower at the edge of time. Scene-to-scene momentum is what keeps a one-day fantasy draft racing forward.

Describing Magic without Confusing the Reader

Magic is at the heart of fantasy—it's the shimmer in the air, the impossible made normal, the heartbeat of your world's wonder. But writing about magic can be tricky. Describe too little, and the reader feels lost or cheated. Describe too much, and your story turns into a rulebook. The key is to make magic *feel* real without slowing the pace or overwhelming the reader with information. When you're writing a fantasy story in one day, you want to keep your flow going. That's where ChatGPT can help you describe spells, magical effects, and strange systems clearly, efficiently, and beautifully—without stopping the story dead in its tracks.

Let's start with what **not** to do: don't over-explain. If a character casts a spell that freezes a river, you don't need three paragraphs about how the energy flows from their chest, down their arm, and into the molecular structure of the water. You just need a vivid image and a sense of consequence. Ask ChatGPT: *"Describe a moment when a mage freezes a river with a single whispered word,"* and you'll get sensory detail, mood, and clarity—all without needing to outline the magic system like a science lecture.

Good magical descriptions often start with the **effect**, not the mechanism. You don't always need to show how the spell works. Just show what happens. Does the room go silent? Does the color drain from the world? Does the character's shadow rise and speak? These kinds of visuals give the reader something to *feel*, even if they don't fully understand what just happened. Use prompts like: *"Describe what it looks and sounds like when a forbidden spell is cast in a cathedral,"* and you'll get atmospheric, emotionally charged writing that does the job fast.

If your story *needs* a more structured system of magic, you can still describe it without dumping everything up front. Use the "iceberg" approach: show the top, suggest the depth. Let characters reference rules in dialogue. Let a failed spell hint at limitations. Let a magical mishap show danger. Ask ChatGPT to help you layer in the magic through action: *"Give me a scene where a young sorcerer tries a levitation spell and it goes wrong,"* and you'll reveal more about the rules of the world through natural storytelling.

Another trick is to use **metaphor and sensory language**. Magic often works better when it's described like emotion or weather. Instead of saying "she channelled energy," say "her veins pulsed with starlight and her fingertips hummed like the strings of a harp." Instead of "a fireball appeared," try "a bead of heat swelled in his palm, growing heavy and furious before it leapt into the air like a furious sun." Ask: *"Describe magic as if it were music,"* or *"What would it feel like to hold lightning in your hand?"* These poetic turns of phrase make the impossible feel tactile and immediate.

Keep an eye on **consistency**. If in your world spells require blood, then every time a character casts one, there should be a cost. If magical objects glow when danger's near, don't forget that detail later. When you're writing fast, like in a one-day sprint, use ChatGPT to track and repeat magical elements: *"List the consistent symptoms of someone who's overused storm magic,"* or *"Describe what casting magic feels like for someone who's afraid of it."* The consistency makes the system believable, even if you don't explain every part.

Use **character reactions** to describe magic. Instead of just saying "the spell worked," show the awe, fear, pain, or delight of the one casting it—or the people watching. You can prompt: *"What might a bystander feel when they see someone raise the dead for the first time?"* or *"Describe a moment of quiet horror when a healing spell revives something it shouldn't have."* These emotions do more to sell the scene than any technical explanation could.

You can also make magic *story-specific*. A healing spell in one scene might be gentle and warm—but if cast by the villain in another, maybe it's painful and controlling. Ask ChatGPT for context-driven versions: *"Describe a love spell cast with regret,"* or *"How would a nature mage's magic differ from a war mage's?"* By shaping the magic around character, mood, and setting, it stops being abstract and becomes part of the story's heartbeat.

Another helpful approach is to limit your **magic vocabulary**. Don't throw ten invented words at the reader in one paragraph. If your story includes custom spell names, magical tools, or mystical laws, introduce them gradually and naturally. Use prompts like: *"How do I explain what a 'soul shard' is without stopping the story?"* ChatGPT might suggest revealing it through dialogue, through action, or through contrast with something the reader already understands.

And if you're stuck trying to describe a magical moment that feels flat or cliché, just ask for alternatives: *"Give me a more original way to describe someone summoning a storm,"* or *"Make this fire spell feel eerie instead of epic."* The AI will give you fresh imagery, new angles, and sometimes a spark that turns the whole scene around.

So remember: the goal isn't to explain everything. It's to create *wonder*. Let magic be strange. Let it be beautiful or terrifying. Let it reflect the character who's wielding it and the world that shaped it. With a few well-chosen lines, a hint of sensory detail, and the help of your AI writing partner, you can make every magical moment land without slowing your pace.

Giving Your Hero an Arc That Feels Earned

At the heart of every great fantasy story is a hero who changes. Maybe they grow stronger, wiser, or braver. Maybe they fail and fall, or learn a painful truth about themselves. But one thing's for sure—their arc has to *feel earned*. No matter how wild your world is, or how magical your story gets, readers crave emotional realism. They want to feel that your protagonist has *become* something by the end that they weren't at the beginning. And when you're writing a fantasy story in a single day, having a clear, meaningful arc mapped out can make your storytelling sharper, more focused, and infinitely more satisfying.

So how do you give your hero a believable arc—especially when time is short and your world is filled with dragons, spells, or gods?

Start with this simple question: **Who are they at the beginning, and who will they be at the end?** That's your arc. Everything in between is how you earn it. Use ChatGPT to help you map it quickly: *"Describe the arc of a cowardly hero who becomes a fearless protector,"* or *"Outline a character journey for someone who learns the truth about their bloodline and chooses their own path instead of fate."* The goal isn't complexity—it's clarity. Know what you're aiming for, and let the story get you there scene by scene.

Now think about **what's holding them back**. Fear. Guilt. Naivety. Pride. These flaws aren't just filler—they're the starting point of change. If your character is afraid of power, give them a situation where power is the only option. If they're selfish, give them someone they can't bear to lose. ChatGPT can help you shape these internal roadblocks: *"What are emotional flaws for a character raised to believe they're superior to everyone else?"* These flaws become your character's personal stakes.

The next step is **pressure**. Change doesn't happen in comfort—it happens when the world pushes. Force your hero into choices. Dilemmas. Sacrifices. They can't grow if nothing tests them. Use prompts like: *"Give me three turning points that challenge a character who hides from responsibility,"* or *"Describe a scene where a hero must choose between saving their friend or completing their mission."* These moments aren't just plot—they're the furnace that forges the arc.

Let your character fail. Let them doubt. Let them backslide. A perfect line from weak to strong is boring. Real arcs zigzag. Readers connect with heroes who struggle, who try and get it wrong, who change their minds and then realize why they can't. Ask ChatGPT: *"What might cause a fantasy hero to question everything they've believed?"* or *"Describe the emotional aftermath of a hero who chooses wrongly in a major battle."*

The **moment of transformation**—the core of the arc—should feel both surprising and inevitable. It's the payoff. It's Frodo standing at the edge of Mount Doom, or Zuko choosing to fight beside Aang. This moment lands best when it echoes what the character feared most in Act I, and when it's earned through all the scenes that came before. Prompt ChatGPT with: *"Create a climax where the hero must reject everything they've wanted to save what they've learned to value,"* or *"What's a symbolic way to show a character finally letting go of guilt?"*

Then there's the **afterward**. What does the hero look like once they've changed? Not in terms of appearance, but in choices, attitude, or perspective. Maybe they return home and walk past the same people they once avoided—but now they stop and help. Maybe they throw away the magical artifact they once craved. Maybe they simply smile in a way they never could before. Ask: *"Show the emotional resolution of a character who now accepts their own power,"* and let that quiet moment say everything.

Your hero's arc doesn't have to be grand. Some of the most powerful transformations are subtle. A character who learns to forgive. To trust. To stop running. To speak their truth. These arcs hit hard when the story supports them at every step—when every trial, every loss, every hard-earned victory has *meant something.*

You can even invert the arc. Maybe your hero *falls*. Maybe they start out full of hope and end jaded. Maybe they betray someone. Maybe they realize they're not the chosen one and hand the torch to someone else. Dark arcs can be just as meaningful if they feel authentic. Prompt ChatGPT: *"Describe the fall of a hero who sacrifices their morals for the greater good,"* and you'll find arcs that resonate beyond simple victory.

And don't forget—fantasy is the perfect genre for **symbolic growth**. Let the arc echo through magic. Maybe your hero's powers shift as they change. Maybe the land itself responds to their transformation. A broken sword reforged. A tattoo that fades as the curse lifts. A ghost that finally stops whispering. These are the poetic echoes of change. You can prompt: *"Give me a magical symbol of a character's emotional transformation,"* or *"Describe a fantasy scene where a character's growth changes the world around them."*

With ChatGPT helping to brainstorm, track, and enrich your character's arc, you don't have to worry about remembering every beat. You just need to keep one truth in mind: your hero should end the story different than they began—not by accident, but because of everything they've experienced.

How to Build a Fantasy Culture in a Few Prompts

Fantasy thrives on the strange, the ancient, and the otherworldly—but it also thrives on *culture*. Not just surface-level stuff like what people wear or how they greet each other, but deep, lived-in traditions, beliefs, values, and contradictions. Culture is what gives your world depth. It's how people live, how they love, what they fear, what they hope for. And if you're writing a fantasy story in a single day, the idea of creating a fully fleshed-out culture might sound impossible—but it's not. You can build a vivid, meaningful culture with just a handful of smart prompts and a little creativity.

The goal isn't to invent everything. The goal is to invent *enough*. Enough to make your world feel unique, to shape how characters behave, and to affect the choices they make. Culture is context. And with ChatGPT at your side, you can build that context in layers—fast, flexible, and fun.

Start simple. Begin with a prompt like:

"Describe a fantasy culture that values silence over speech," or

"Invent a desert-dwelling society that worships the stars."

These kinds of prompts immediately give you an anchor—something to build around. In response, you'll get ideas for beliefs, rituals, clothing, and maybe even phrases or holidays.

From there, go deeper by asking about **social structure**. Who holds power? Why? Is it a monarchy, a council, a theocracy, a system where power changes hands every lunar cycle? Try:

"What type of leadership would emerge in a society that fears individual fame?" or

"How would a matriarchal forest society choose its leaders?"

This gives you insight into politics, family structures, and how your characters might view status or destiny.

Then ask about **daily life**. How do people eat, work, rest, love, and celebrate? You can ask:

"Describe the daily routine of a villager in a high-altitude mountain culture," or

"What are traditional courtship rituals in a culture that treats dreams as sacred?"

These answers generate not just colorful moments, but also character-specific detail that you can drop naturally into dialogue and scenes.

Next up: **beliefs and taboos**. These are often what shape the tension in a story. What do people believe in this world? What are they forbidden to do?

Ask ChatGPT:

"What are some taboos in a culture that believes time is sacred?" or

"What myths might exist in a culture where children are born with magical marks?"

These beliefs help shape the stakes of your story and influence how your characters will be judged, praised, or punished by their society.

You can also bring culture to life through **language and phrases**. You don't need to create an entire fantasy language—just a few sayings, curses, or blessings can do the trick. Try:

"Give me ten idioms from a sea-faring culture," or

"What would a blessing sound like in a culture that reveres fire?"

These small touches instantly signal a unique worldview. A character who curses by saying, "By the bones of the drowned," tells you a lot about the society they come from.

Another angle? **Art and beauty.** Every culture has a different idea of what's beautiful, sacred, or valuable. Maybe scars are considered symbols of spiritual progress. Maybe music is forbidden during daylight. Maybe poetry is currency. Ask:

"How might a culture express grief if they're forbidden from crying?" or

"What kind of clothing would be worn by a people who believe the moon sees all?"

Details like these help build scenes that are emotionally rich and visually distinct.

If your world includes multiple cultures—and most good fantasy worlds do—you can quickly define contrasts with questions like:

"How would two neighboring cultures differ in their view of death?" or

"What would trade look like between a nomadic magical culture and an underground mining civilization?"

These contrasts set up tension, diplomacy, prejudice, or alliances—perfect story fuel.

One trick to keep things fast is to work from **theme**. If your story is about power, ask:

"Describe a culture where magic is distributed based on ancestry."

If your story is about isolation, ask:

"What kind of traditions would evolve in a walled-off city that hasn't seen outsiders in generations?"

This keeps your worldbuilding tied to your story's emotional core.

And don't forget **ceremony**—marriages, births, funerals, coming-of-age rites. These moments create opportunities for drama, character growth, or shocking interruptions. You can ask:

"Describe a coming-of-age ceremony in a sky-worshipping culture," or

"What happens during a funeral in a society where souls are believed to be reborn in storms?"

Ceremonial scenes are often perfect set pieces—full of visuals, meaning, and potential for plot twists.

The magic of using prompts to build culture is that you're not guessing in the dark. You're collaborating. You're co-creating a world with logic, feeling, and flair—and doing it quickly, without getting bogged down in worldbuilding that never makes it onto the page.

So next time you need a culture that feels real in a world of impossible things, ask a few smart questions. Focus on beliefs, customs, structure, beauty, and language. And let ChatGPT help you layer your world like a tapestry—one thread at a time.

Next, we'll turn to **how to write fantasy scenes that blend action with emotion**, so you can create battles, chases, and magical duels that hit the heart as well as the eye.

Politics and Power Struggles in Fantasy Realms

Fantasy isn't just fireballs and flying beasts—it's thrones, oaths, betrayals, and whispered threats behind closed doors. Power is at the heart of every kingdom, every rebellion, every empire that ever fell. It's who holds it, who wants it, and what they're willing to do to keep it. Politics in fantasy gives your world structure and tension. It defines alliances, drives wars, and creates opportunities for betrayal, ambition, and uneasy partnerships. And the best part? You don't need to write a 10-book epic to do it. With the right focus—and a little help from ChatGPT—you can weave gripping political dynamics into your one-day fantasy story with clarity and speed.

First, remember that fantasy politics doesn't have to mean endless council meetings or royal decrees. At its core, politics is just power in motion. Someone has it. Someone wants it. And someone's willing to risk everything to change the balance. Start with a prompt like:

"Describe a power struggle between three noble houses in a crumbling kingdom," or

"What kind of political tension might exist in a city ruled by a magical elite?"

This will give you a web of players, motives, and possible flashpoints—all without needing a full history book.

Decide what kind of government your world runs on. Is it a monarchy? A republic? A theocracy ruled by priests who claim to speak for a god? Maybe power is based on bloodlines, magical ability, or even age. You can prompt:

"Create a fantasy political system where only dreamers are allowed to lead," or

"Design a society where magic users are outlawed, but secretly control the government."

This helps ground the conflict in your world's rules—and gives your characters reasons to defy, manipulate, or break them.

Then look at **who benefits** and **who suffers**. That's where your tension lives. If one city gets all the water while others die of thirst, resentment builds. If nobles hoard magic while peasants are forbidden from learning spells, rebellion brews. Ask ChatGPT:

"What social tensions might exist in a kingdom where healing magic is only available to the wealthy?"

or

"Describe a political system where a council of oracles controls policy through prophecy."

These structures give you instant stakes and ready-made sources of conflict.

Power struggles can be large-scale—wars between kingdoms—or intimate—two siblings vying for control of a family legacy. You can prompt:

"Describe a secret rivalry between two royal heirs," or

"Give me a political conflict between a village elder and a charismatic outsider."

These smaller battles are perfect for keeping the focus tight in a one-day story while still giving the plot emotional weight.

Corruption is another great engine for fantasy politics. It might be magical—like a cursed crown that makes rulers paranoid—or it might be all too human. Greed, fear, ambition.

You can ask ChatGPT:

"What's a subtle form of magical corruption that influences policy?"

or

"Describe a ruling council where every member has a secret that can be used against them."

Now you have room for blackmail, shifting alliances, and betrayals that change everything.

Don't forget the **underdogs**. Rebels, secret orders, disenfranchised groups. Fantasy thrives on the tension between those in power and those who refuse to accept the rules. Ask:

"Create a resistance movement in a kingdom where art is banned," or

"What would a secret guild of rogue mages look like in a city that hunts spellcasters?"

This gives you characters with goals, desperation, and a reason to disrupt the status quo.

Use dialogue to show political tension without stopping the story for exposition. A barbed exchange between two nobles. A cryptic warning from a priest. A speech from a rebel leader. Prompt ChatGPT:

"Write a tense dinner conversation between a queen and her traitorous advisor," or

"Give me a coded message passed between two spies in a magical court."

Politics doesn't have to be delivered in monologues—it lives in glances, gestures, and what's left unsaid.

If your story has a prophecy, a magical heir, or a legendary weapon, you've already got built-in political weight. Who controls the prophecy? Who believes in it? Who wants to twist it? Try asking:

"Describe the political fallout in a realm where a child is born with the mark of an ancient ruler," or

"What happens when multiple factions claim ownership of a weapon of legend?"

Suddenly your character isn't just in a personal journey—they're at the heart of a power storm.

And let's not forget **consequences**. Power plays aren't just drama—they should change the course of events. If a general betrays their king, armies move. If a treaty is broken, magic might react violently. If a throne is taken by force, the gods themselves might curse the land. Use prompts like:

"What are the magical consequences of breaking a royal oath?" or

"How does a kingdom fracture when a peace agreement is undone by lies?"

Your politics should feel like a living system—when someone pulls a string, something else snaps.

You don't need endless detail. One kingdom. One conspiracy. One betrayal. That's enough to power an entire story. ChatGPT can help you keep the pace brisk while still delivering high-impact politics by giving you focused moments, smart twists, and believable tensions. Use it to brainstorm schemes, flesh out power players, or generate a backstabbing alliance on the spot.

So yes—your story can have sword fights, monsters, and magical duels. But never forget that sometimes, the most dangerous thing in a fantasy world isn't a dragon. It's a smiling noble with a knife behind their back and a title to lose.

Rebellion, and Quest: Choosing Your Fantasy Plot Core

Every fantasy story needs a heart—a reason the journey begins, a fire that drives the characters forward, a thread that weaves through every scene. That's your plot core. And in fantasy, three plot types reign supreme: **war**, **rebellion**, and **quest**. You'll see them everywhere from *The Lord of the Rings* to *Game of Thrones*, from *The Hunger Games* to *The Witcher*. These plot cores aren't just popular—they're incredibly flexible. Each one offers built-in stakes, emotional depth, and endless room for magic, monsters, and mayhem. And when you're writing a fantasy story in a single day, choosing a clear core helps keep your focus sharp and your pacing tight.

So how do you decide which plot core is right for your story?

Let's start with the **war story**. This is about nations colliding, armies clashing, and worlds breaking under the weight of violence. War plots often feature multiple perspectives: rulers making impossible decisions, soldiers on the front lines, spies in enemy cities, and civilians trying to survive the fallout. The emotional core of a war story usually revolves around loyalty, sacrifice, loss, and the price of power.

To build a war-driven story quickly, ask ChatGPT:

"Describe a fantasy war between a magical empire and a nomadic people who control the skies," or

"What might drive two ancient kingdoms to war over a sacred river?"

From that seed, you get your backdrop, your stakes, and a battlefield for your characters to fight on—physically, morally, emotionally.

Next is **rebellion**—the story of the underdog rising up. This plot is about oppression, injustice, and the people who fight back. It can be epic or intimate. Maybe your story follows a single rebel smuggling messages through cursed tunnels, or a band of freedom fighters leading a revolution in the capital city. Rebellion plots are personal. Your hero isn't just fighting for survival—they're fighting for a better world.

Rebellion stories give you clear sides and shifting loyalties. Use ChatGPT to prompt scenes like:

"Write the first meeting between a reluctant rebel leader and a spy from the enemy," or

"Describe a rebellion that began as a religious movement but became something darker."

Rebellion brings a great balance of action, political tension, and character growth. It also naturally gives you emotional arcs: betrayal, unity, desperation, hope.

Then there's the **quest**. The most classic of all fantasy plot cores, the quest story is about a journey—physical and emotional. It could be a search for a magical relic, a journey to awaken a sleeping god, or an attempt to reach a mythical city before it vanishes. Quest stories are simple in structure but limitless in content. You can pack in creatures, maps, riddles, cursed lands, ancient guardians, and a ticking clock.

The best quests aren't just about the goal—they're about how the journey changes the people on it. Ask ChatGPT for help like:

"Describe a quest to retrieve an item that doesn't want to be found," or

"Give me obstacles for a group of strangers traveling through a land that erases memories."

With just a few prompts, you can outline your quest's stages—departure, trials, crisis, and return—and let your characters grow along the way.

So how do you choose between war, rebellion, and quest?

Ask yourself what your **protagonist needs to overcome**. If they need to face grief, trauma, or the weight of past sins, maybe a war story will reflect that scale. If they need to find their voice, defy tradition, or change their world, rebellion is a great fit. If they need to grow, face the unknown, and discover something about themselves, the quest is your best path.

You can also mix them. A rebellion may start during a war. A quest might trigger political upheaval. A kingdom may be at war, while your hero sneaks off on a personal mission to find the only weapon that can end the conflict. Use ChatGPT to ask:

"How can I combine a rebellion plot with a secret quest?" or

"What personal journey might mirror a larger war in a fantasy setting?"

Whichever you choose, make sure the core drives the rest of the story. Every subplot, every piece of worldbuilding, every spell and swordfight should in some way connect back to that central thread. When in doubt, ask: *Does this moment move the war forward? Deepen the rebellion? Take the quest one step closer?* If it doesn't, cut it—or make it work harder.

One great technique for keeping the story tight is using **milestones**. For a war plot, that might be a lost battle, a surprise alliance, a captured city. For a rebellion, it might be the first act of defiance, the rallying of allies, the betrayal that threatens everything. For a quest, it might be the first trial, the midpoint twist, the moment where the hero almost turns back. Ask ChatGPT:

"Give me five key story beats for a rebellion plot," or

"Outline a quest story with an emotional arc tied to a lost sibling."

These beats keep your pacing clean and give you momentum from start to finish.

So whether your story marches to the drums of war, the chants of rebellion, or the call of the open road, make your plot core clear, compelling, and emotionally charged. That's what pulls readers through your world—one battle, one broken chain, or one step at a time.

Next, we'll dive into **building emotional scenes that matter**, so your story doesn't just dazzle with magic—but lingers because of heart.

Love in the Realm of Dragons: Writing Romance in Fantasy

There's something unforgettable about romance in fantasy. Maybe it's the intensity of two people finding each other amid chaos. Maybe it's the tension of love blooming in a world full of curses, crowns, and ancient prophecies. Or maybe it's just that when magic is real, so is the possibility that love could be the strongest force of all—even stronger than fire-breathing dragons. Whether your story is about epic battles or quiet journeys, weaving in romance can elevate the emotional depth of your fantasy tale. And when you're writing a fantasy story in one day, a well-executed romance gives you instant chemistry, conflict, and catharsis.

The key is to make the romance feel earned, not forced. It doesn't matter if your lovers are star-crossed royals or rival spell-casters who can't stand each other until they do. What matters is that their connection grows organically from who they are and what they're going through. Fantasy is about transformation—and so is love. That makes them natural allies in storytelling.

Start by deciding how central the romance is to your story. Is it the main plot, a subplot, or a background thread? If you're doing a quest, maybe it starts as subtle flirtation that deepens with each shared danger. In a rebellion story, maybe your lovers are on opposite sides, forced to choose between heart and cause. Ask ChatGPT:

"Describe a romance that develops between two warriors during a magical civil war," or

"Create a slow-burn romance between a healer and a cursed prince during a journey."

This gives you a dynamic starting point you can build on while staying within your main story arc.

Great fantasy romance starts with **chemistry**, and chemistry starts with conflict. Don't make them perfect for each other. Make them *compelling*. Maybe one is bound by honor and the other lives by instinct. Maybe one is running from fate and the other is chasing it. Use prompts like:

"What kind of tension might exist between a mage who fears their power and a lover who wants them to use it?"

or

"Describe a fantasy relationship where one character has been ordered to kill the other."

The best romantic arcs put emotional obstacles in the way—and then tear them down, brick by brick.

Dialogue is your secret weapon. A romantic scene doesn't need to be a declaration. It can be an argument that slips into vulnerability. A joke that masks fear. A simple act of care during a moment of pain.

Ask ChatGPT to help:

"Write a fantasy scene where two characters bond over their scars," or

"Create a moment of intimacy between a runaway noble and a desert guide while hiding from enemies."

These smaller beats build trust and tension—and make the payoff land harder.

Fantasy romance is also about **setting**. The environments you place your characters in affect how love feels. A conversation by a moonlit lake of spirits hits different than one in a war tent with blood on the floor. You can make romance feel epic or intimate just by choosing the right moment and place.

Use prompts like:

"Describe a romantic moment between two characters inside a crumbling tower as a storm rages outside," or

"Write a scene where a character confesses love while suspended between two floating islands."

This is where fantasy shines—you get to turn emotion into spectacle without losing sincerity.

You can also layer in **magical stakes**. Maybe one lover is immortal and the other is cursed to forget. Maybe their bond is the key to saving the kingdom—or the thing that might destroy it. These stakes raise the emotional investment. Ask:

"What's a magical consequence of two soul-bound characters falling out of sync?" or

"Describe a magical bond that causes physical pain when the lovers lie to each other."

When love itself has power in your world, readers will lean in.

Don't forget to let the romance change your characters. Just like a hero grows through their arc, love should challenge and transform them. A cold-hearted warrior who learns to feel again. A skeptical loner who lets someone in. A royal who stops pretending. Ask ChatGPT:

"How might falling in love force a character to question their loyalty?"

or

"Describe the emotional arc of a character who believes they're unworthy of love but finds it anyway."

These arcs hit hard when paired with action and adventure.

Fantasy romance doesn't have to end happily—but it should end with meaning. Maybe one character lets the other go for the greater good. Maybe they're reunited in the epilogue after years apart. Or maybe they're together, scarred but whole, looking out over a new dawn. Use prompts like:

"Describe a bittersweet goodbye between lovers who saved the world but can't be together," or

"Write a final scene where two characters find peace in each other after the battle."

Even if your story is short or written quickly, the emotions can linger.

So whether it's a fire-lit kiss before the final stand, a stolen glance across enemy lines, or a love letter hidden in a book of forbidden spells—let your fantasy romance feel alive. Let it breathe, clash, surprise, and heal. Because in a world of dragons, gods, and crumbling empires, love may be the most human magic of all.

Integrating Mystery and Intrigue into Your Plot

Fantasy doesn't have to be all swords, dragons, and magical duels—it can whisper, deceive, and lead the reader down twisting corridors full of secrets. That's where **mystery and intrigue** come in. We're not just talking about whodunits or locked-room puzzles. In a fantasy world, mystery can mean ancient ruins humming with forgotten power, a masked noble who never eats in public, or a prophecy with a missing verse. Intrigue is the art of keeping readers—and characters—uncertain, curious, and suspicious. It creates tension that simmers rather than explodes, and when done right, it makes every choice and every moment feel loaded.

The good news is you don't need to change your entire story to use mystery. You just need to **layer it in**. With ChatGPT as your writing ally, you can generate plot twists, hidden motives, secret histories, and cryptic clues quickly, without pausing your story's momentum. And in a one-day writing sprint, those layers can make your fantasy tale feel bigger, deeper, and more alive.

Let's start with a simple idea: **someone knows something they're not saying**. That's the seed of mystery. It might be a king with a locked room, a priest who edits the sacred texts, or a soldier who survived a battle they shouldn't have. Ask ChatGPT:

"Give me a character with a secret that could collapse the kingdom," or

"Describe a magical order that only speaks in riddles."

From there, you've got a thread to pull. And once you start pulling it, the story starts to unravel in the best way.

One powerful mystery device is the **missing piece**. A stolen artifact. A page ripped from a book. A prophecy that ends too early. These gaps suggest something important is hidden—and someone wants it that way. Use prompts like:

"Describe a legend about a vanished city that no map dares to mark," or

"Create a mystery involving a spell no one remembers how to cast."

This creates instant intrigue without needing to invent a new plot—it adds flavor to the one you're already telling.

Symbols and clues are essential to mystery in fantasy. Maybe it's a recurring dream. A tattoo seen in every kingdom. A phrase etched into the walls of ancient temples. These elements invite both characters and readers to start piecing things together. Ask:

"What's a cryptic message left behind by a dying oracle?" or

"Create a pattern of magical events that form a hidden warning."

These tools make your world feel layered with meaning, even if you don't explain everything right away.

Intrigue also comes from **character motives**. Not everyone wants the same thing—and even allies can hide agendas. Use ChatGPT to spice things up:

"Give me a noble who supports the hero but secretly wants them to fail," or

"Describe a healer who's been hiding their true identity for years."

When readers can't trust everyone, every scene gains tension.

Mystery often thrives on **what isn't said**. Suspicious silences. Contradictory stories. Inconsistencies that go unnoticed by most—but not your protagonist. You can use dialogue to plant seeds:

"Strange," said the captain, "I could've sworn the statue faced the other way yesterday."

A small line like that can shift the entire mood. Ask ChatGPT for subtleties:

"Write a scene where a character realizes a small detail doesn't match the story they've been told."

These moments spark the reader's imagination—and suspicion.

Fantasy is the perfect genre for **hidden histories**. Maybe magic used to be something else. Maybe the gods the people worship aren't the real ones. Maybe the founding heroes weren't heroes at all. Prompt ChatGPT:

"What's a hidden truth behind a kingdom's founding legend?" or

"Describe an artifact believed to be holy that holds a dark secret."

These revelations can drive whole arcs, or just add richness to your world.

You can also integrate **investigation subplots** into your main story. Your hero might be solving a murder in the middle of a war, or uncovering corruption while on a quest. Think of it like a thread running alongside the action. It slows nothing—it just deepens everything. Ask:

"What clues might a character find in a burned-out magical library?" or

"Create an intrigue subplot involving a missing prince whose death was faked."

And don't forget to use **mystery to reflect theme**. If your story is about trust, make betrayal a mystery. If it's about identity, hide the truth about a character's origin. If it's about fate, leave the prophecy unclear. Ask ChatGPT:

"How can I build a mystery around a character who was never supposed to exist?" or

"Design a twist where the villain is the only one who knows the truth about the world."

The payoff is everything. When you do reveal the secret, let it *change something*. It should reshape the reader's understanding of the story—or of the characters. It doesn't have to be shocking. It just has to *matter*. ChatGPT can help build these moments:

"Write a revelation scene where the hero discovers their mentor was part of the enemy all along," or

"Describe a twist where the magical cure turns out to be the original curse."

In fantasy, mystery doesn't just entertain—it enriches. It makes your world feel older, stranger, and more alive. And even in a single day of writing, a well-placed secret or a cleverly buried truth can elevate your story from exciting to unforgettable.

Pacing the Adventure So It Never Drags

In fantasy, it's easy to get swept up in your worldbuilding—lost in sprawling kingdoms, tangled in prophecies, or wandering too long through an enchanted forest of exposition. But readers don't follow your story just to admire the scenery—they follow the *movement*. Pacing is what keeps your fantasy tale alive. It's the rhythm of tension and release, of action and quiet, of discovery and payoff. A story with strong pacing feels like a ride—fast when it needs to be, still when it should be, but always moving. And when you're writing your fantasy adventure in a single day, nailing that pace will help you write faster, smarter, and better.

Let's start with the simplest truth: **every scene must do something.** It has to move the plot forward, deepen a character, raise a question, or deliver a reveal. If it doesn't do any of those, cut it—or reshape it. Ask ChatGPT:

"Does this scene deepen character or drive plot? If not, how can I add tension or purpose?"

A conversation becomes sharper if it hides a secret. A travel scene gains value if it includes a choice or discovery. Nothing should be idle, even if it's quiet.

Now think in terms of **beats**—those key moments that guide your story's rhythm. Every story has its high points and low points: the opening hook, the inciting incident, the midpoint twist, the dark night of the soul, and the climax. When you're plotting quickly, it helps to see your story like a series of these signposts. Prompt ChatGPT with:

"Give me five major plot beats for a fast-paced fantasy quest," or

"What's the pacing breakdown of a three-act fantasy structure?"

You'll get a scaffold that shows where the energy should rise, hold, and explode.

To avoid dragging, you need to **control your exposition**. Fantasy is notorious for overexplaining—systems of magic, lineage charts, the political history of the Dry Winds of Aruun. Resist the urge to dump. Instead, feed the worldbuilding in through dialogue, action, and setting. Ask:

"How do I deliver lore through conflict instead of explanation?"

Use mystery. Use hints. Let your characters learn as the reader does. If something can be explained later, wait. And if it doesn't matter? Cut it.

Another great pacing trick is to build with **mini-cliffhangers**. You don't need every chapter to end in an explosion—but end with a question, a twist, a choice. Something unresolved. It keeps readers turning pages. Try asking ChatGPT:

"Suggest five chapter endings for a fantasy story that keep tension high," or

"What kind of turning point should hit halfway through a story about a stolen spellbook?"

These help you keep the suspense alive without needing a massive plot twist every few pages.

Use **action wisely**. Too much, and it gets exhausting. Too little, and your story feels flat. Action should change something: a power shift, a revelation, a cost. Even a small moment—like a confrontation in a tavern—should create consequences.

Ask:

"How do I balance action with emotional stakes in a fantasy duel?"

Because when action is tied to character, it feels urgent. When it's just noise, it drags—even if it's loud.

Likewise, don't fear **quiet scenes**—but make them count. A slow scene can reveal inner conflict, deepen relationships, or plant something that explodes later. A calm before the storm works when the storm *matters*. You can prompt ChatGPT with:

"Give me ideas for quiet fantasy scenes that still build tension," or

"What emotional beat can follow a major battle to keep the pace steady but meaningful?"

Think of your pacing like breathing—inhale tension, exhale emotion.

Transitions between scenes matter too. Don't wander. Keep momentum tight. Instead of, "Three days later, they reached the mountains," you could write, "By the time the mountains appeared, their map was soaked in blood and the horses refused to go further." That sentence still moves time forward—but gives you mood, tension, and a reason to keep reading. Use ChatGPT for bridge moments:

"Write a paragraph that transitions from a forest escape to a castle negotiation without losing momentum."

Chapter length also plays a part in pacing. Shorter chapters feel faster. Longer ones feel slower, but can offer depth. You can use this to your advantage. Right before a major twist, make chapters shorter to tighten the tension. After, let them breathe to absorb the fallout. Ask:

"How do I adjust chapter pacing to increase suspense?"

ChatGPT can help you structure your scenes for max impact.

And don't forget to **escalate**. Your stakes should climb. Each act should feel more intense than the last. A minor scuffle becomes a full chase. A strange encounter becomes a deadly alliance. A stolen object becomes the key to the kingdom's ruin. Ask:

"What are three ways to raise the stakes in the second half of a fantasy novel?"

Keep layering—tension, consequence, and urgency—and your story won't drag because it can't.

Finally, always know where you're heading. If you're stuck, slow, or unsure, prompt yourself with:

"What needs to happen next to bring my hero closer to their goal—or further from it?"

That one question keeps your pacing honest. When every scene either builds toward the climax or complicates it, your story pulses forward like a heartbeat.

So yes—fantasy can be sprawling, rich, and full of lore. But pacing is what turns it from a still painting into a living journey. With a few smart decisions, a couple of strong beats, and ChatGPT's support as your pace-partner, you can write a fantasy story that races, breathes, and roars from beginning to end.

Emotional Highs and Lows: Writing Powerful Moments

Fantasy may be built on dragons, spells, and legendary quests—but what readers truly remember are the *moments*. That one line of dialogue that breaks the hero. The reunion that comes after all hope is lost. The heartbreak that no magic can undo. These are the **emotional highs and lows** of your story—the beating heart beneath the worldbuilding. They don't just enrich your fantasy narrative; they *anchor* it. And when you're writing your entire story in a single day, knowing how to hit these moments with clarity and force gives your writing the kind of emotional depth that lingers long after the last scene fades.

Powerful emotional moments come from contrast. Just like pacing needs tension and release, emotion needs *build-up and payoff*. If your character is constantly devastated, readers grow numb. If they're always triumphant, the wins start to feel empty. The magic is in the movement—hope followed by heartbreak, triumph shadowed by loss, stillness shattered by a confession. And to create that rhythm quickly, you can use ChatGPT as both brainstorming partner and emotional barometer.

Let's start with the **emotional low**—often the story's turning point. This is the moment your character breaks. They lose someone. They fail. They realize they were wrong. It's the cave before the climb. You can prompt ChatGPT with:

"Write a scene where a hero is rejected by the person they were trying to save," or

"Describe the moment a warrior realizes their legendary victory came at the wrong cost."

These are the scenes where tears hit the page. The silence is heavier. The magic fades, or becomes something cruel.

But don't stop at sadness. Dig into **emotional contradiction**. Grief tangled with relief. Rage interrupted by guilt. Love shadowed by fear. That complexity makes moments stick. Ask:

"Describe a fantasy scene where a character achieves their goal but feels emptier than ever," or

"Write a conversation where two allies comfort each other while hiding their real pain."

Let your characters *wrestle* with emotion, not just express it. That's where the rawness lives.

Now flip it. Go to the **emotional high**—the moment of victory, connection, revelation. But again, make it specific. A reunion only matters if the characters were truly torn apart. A victory only hits hard if it came at a cost. Ask ChatGPT:

"Write a reunion scene between two siblings thought to be dead," or

"Describe a magical healing that restores someone's body—but not their memory."

You can craft joy that's tinged with sorrow, or triumph that feels earned, not convenient.

One of the strongest ways to elevate emotional highs is with **contrast**. After a brutal loss, a simple kindness becomes radiant. After betrayal, a shared joke feels like grace. Use the rhythm of your story to make these moments shine brighter. Ask ChatGPT:

"Give me a sequence where a hopeless hero is reminded of why they must go on," or

"Write a quiet scene of joy between two characters surrounded by war."

Dialogue is another key tool. People don't always say exactly what they feel—but what they *do* say reveals volumes. A character who says, "You're late," instead of "I thought you were dead," or who quietly returns an item they once stole—those are the lines that punch the gut. Ask for nuance:

"Write a conversation where one character confesses love without saying 'I love you,'" or

"Describe a farewell where both characters pretend it's not goodbye."

These lines don't need a trumpet. They need *truth*.

Use your fantasy elements to *amplify* emotion, not distract from it. A love confession during a magical eclipse. A funeral where the stars fall. A spell that fails because the caster can't let go. Ask:

"Describe an emotional climax involving a character's last use of magic," or

"What does grief look like in a world where souls are visible after death?"

These moments show that magic and emotion aren't separate—they enhance each other when handled with care.

Symbolism also strengthens emotional resonance. A crown laid on an empty throne. A sword driven into the earth instead of a heart. A flower blooming from a grave. Ask ChatGPT for ideas like:

"What symbolic gesture could a warrior make to show forgiveness without speaking?" or

"Describe a magical object that fades as a character loses hope."

And remember that emotional impact doesn't have to be dramatic. Some of the strongest moments are the quietest. A character watches a sunrise for the first time in years. They say the name of someone they've never been allowed to mourn. They let go of something they swore they'd never release. These scenes don't shout—but they echo. Use prompts like:

"Write a quiet emotional scene with no dialogue but full of meaning," or

"Describe a moment where a character chooses peace over revenge."

When writing fast, let your instincts lead. You don't need to build emotional intensity into every scene. You just need a few moments where everything *lands*. Where the reader feels what the character feels—whether that's joy, heartbreak, fear, or love. With ChatGPT's help, you can shape those moments quickly, revise them to sharpen the sting or the sweetness, and move forward without losing momentum.

Because in the end, magic makes fantasy shine—but *emotion* is what makes it unforgettable.

When to Show, When to Tell in a Fantasy Setting

"Show, don't tell" is one of the most famous pieces of writing advice—and in fantasy, it's both powerful and potentially paralyzing. You're building entire worlds from scratch, inventing magic systems, kingdoms, species, histories, and belief systems. If you tried to *show* all of that detail through action and description alone, you'd need a thousand pages just to explain where the floating islands come from. But if you *only tell*, your story might feel like a history lesson instead of an adventure. So the real question isn't whether to show or tell—it's **when** to do each.

In a one-day writing sprint, making smart choices about when to show and when to tell is essential. It helps you keep your momentum, focus on what matters, and deliver immersive storytelling without overloading your reader. Fortunately, with a fantasy story, you have the freedom to blend these approaches creatively—and with the help of ChatGPT, you can make those choices quickly and with precision.

Let's break it down.

Show when emotion is high.

This is where you want the reader to *feel* what the character is going through. When your hero stands on the battlefield, don't just say "She was scared." Show the tremble in her fingers, the cold sweat under her armor, the way she clenched her sword like it was a lifeline. Ask ChatGPT:

"Write a scene showing a character trying to hide their fear before a duel,"

and you'll get behavior, physicality, and tension instead of just a label.

Showing is also vital during **pivotal character interactions**. A betrayal, a confession, a first meeting with a dragon god—these are moments to draw out, to make the reader live inside them. You can prompt ChatGPT:

"Show a conversation where one character realizes the other is lying,"

and it'll use silence, gestures, clipped words, and reactions to build emotional subtext.

Tell when it's not worth slowing down.

Sometimes you need to move fast. If your story jumps forward a few days while your characters travel, you don't need to describe every rock and tree. You can write, "They crossed the sun-scorched plains with few words and even fewer signs of pursuit," and be done. Ask ChatGPT:

"Summarize a three-day journey across a cursed desert in two sentences,"

and you'll get something lean but vivid.

You can also *tell* when you're conveying background information or context. Fantasy readers expect some telling—they know they're being dropped into a new world. The trick is to make it *interesting* and keep it short. Instead of dumping the full history of the Thousand-Year War, try:

"For ten centuries, the North and South waged quiet war, not with swords, but with storms. Only now had the skies gone still."

If you need help condensing lore without sounding like a textbook, prompt ChatGPT:

"Write one paragraph of fantasy backstory that reads like a myth or legend."

A helpful rule: **show for drama, tell for context.**

If the reader needs to understand *how* something works—like a magical tax, or why everyone's afraid of the old bridge—you can tell them directly in one or two lines. But if someone's trying to cross that bridge at night, and it starts whispering their name? Now you show.

Another trick: **show the symptom, tell the cause.**

For example, you show that a character clutches their wrist every time someone says "The Hollow King." Later, you tell: "He'd escaped that dungeon, but the brand still burned when he remembered." You've earned the telling *because* the showing came first. ChatGPT can help you build these layers:

"Write a scene showing a magical curse affecting a character's behavior, followed by a line explaining its origin."

Fantasy allows you to blur the line between showing and telling by using **stylized exposition**. Characters might speak in proverbs, myths, or prayers. A bard might sing the tale. A temple might paint it on the wall. Use worldbuilding itself as your narrative device. Prompt:

"Show the legend of a fallen star through the eyes of a child visiting a shrine,"

and you're telling and showing at the same time.

Here's where showing often fails—when you overdescribe things that don't matter. You don't need to show a full bartering scene unless something important happens during it. Don't show someone eating soup unless the spoon is poisoned or the tension is unbearable. Ask yourself: *What changes in this scene?* If the answer is "nothing," then tell it—or skip it.

And here's where telling falls short—when you try to *tell emotion*. "He was angry." "She was in love." "They were afraid." These statements aren't wrong—but they're weak on their own. Use them as a frame, then *show* what that looks like. Try:

"She was afraid. She kept her eyes on the floor, as if the wrong glance might turn her to stone."

You can also ask ChatGPT to balance for you:

"Convert this passage from telling to showing,"

or

"Write this action sequence with emotional depth instead of just movement."

This lets you edit your draft on the fly and keep the emotional resonance strong.

Ultimately, good fantasy writing blends showing and telling like magic and steel—each sharp, each necessary. Show what readers need to *feel*. Tell what they need to *know*. Trust them to imagine the rest.

Using ChatGPT to Write Fast but Stay Creative

When you're racing the clock to write a full fantasy story in a single day, speed matters—but so does imagination. Writing fast shouldn't mean writing bland. It's not about cutting corners; it's about removing friction. That's where ChatGPT becomes your secret weapon. With the right approach, you can use AI to keep ideas flowing, fix roadblocks in real time, and explore creative paths you wouldn't have thought of on your own. You get the momentum of a sprint *and* the magic of spontaneity. So let's talk about how to use ChatGPT to write fast—and stay wildly, relentlessly creative in the process.

It all starts with **knowing what to ask**. ChatGPT can generate pages of text, but the real power is in the prompts. Instead of saying "Write my fantasy story," say:

"Give me five plot twists for a story about a mage who's afraid of their own power."

or

"Describe a magical duel that reveals a character's secret."

These micro-prompts give you precise, usable content. You don't have to wade through fluff—you get sparks that keep your creative engine running.

Want to write even faster? Use ChatGPT to **outline before you draft**. Just five minutes of planning can save you hours of rewriting. Try this:

"Give me a three-act fantasy story structure involving a cursed forest, a reluctant hero, and a hidden prophecy."

Now you've got a roadmap. With each beat in place, you can focus on telling the story instead of figuring out what comes next.

And if you're stuck mid-draft, don't stare at the screen—*ask something.*

"What happens when a character opens a door they were told never to touch?"

"What's a magical consequence of telling a lie in this world?"

Even one line of response can unlock a whole new scene. This isn't about ChatGPT taking over your writing. It's about it keeping your momentum alive.

Use the AI to **fill in your worldbuilding** without slowing down. Need a city name? A weird festival? A historical conflict that shaped the land? You can type:

"What's a strange winter tradition in a mountain-dwelling magical society?"

or

"Give me a political feud between two houses that once fought over a dragon egg."

These details make your world feel deep—but you don't have to spend hours inventing them from scratch.

Also, use ChatGPT to **build character layers fast**. Don't write a bio—just ask:

"What secret might a noble sorcerer be hiding from their apprentice?"

"Describe a fantasy character who smiles every time they lie."

These little sparks turn flat ideas into dynamic characters you actually want to write.

If your prose is feeling flat or repetitive, use ChatGPT to **punch it up**.

You can say:

"Rewrite this paragraph with more emotion,"

or

"Make this scene more tense and poetic."

This helps you maintain voice, rhythm, and depth without stopping your forward motion. Think of it like a second brain feeding you better word choices while you sprint.

ChatGPT can also help you **stay fresh when fatigue hits**. Midway through a one-day draft, your creativity might dip. Instead of pushing through dull scenes, use a prompt to reenergize.

"Give me a twist that changes everything halfway through a quest,"

or

"Describe a moment of unexpected magic that interrupts a tense argument."

Suddenly, you're not just writing to hit your word count—you're surprising yourself again.

You can even use it to **track your emotional beats**. Ask:

"What's a quiet, powerful moment for a character who just experienced a major loss?"

or

"Give me an emotional turning point for a character who's finally found the truth."

This keeps your fantasy story grounded in feeling, even when the plot's moving fast.

And here's something crucial: **you're still the writer**. ChatGPT is your assistant, your brainstorming partner, your pressure release valve. It's not about handing over the story. It's about clearing out the mental clutter so your best ideas can shine. You choose what to use, what to rewrite, and what to ignore.

If you're writing dialogue and it feels stiff, try:

"Write a tense exchange between a reluctant hero and a mercenary who's losing patience."

You'll get rhythm, flow, and tone you can adapt on the spot. If you need to name ten taverns in ten seconds, ask. If you want your descriptions to feel more sensory or strange, ask. The beauty of using ChatGPT is that it's always ready—and always fast.

One last trick: **don't just use it to fix problems. Use it to challenge yourself.**

Try:

"Give me a story beat where the hero fails—and it makes things better."

or

"What's the most unexpected but logical twist I could add right now?"

This turns ChatGPT into more than a writing tool. It becomes your partner in narrative risk, helping you push past your habits and into bold new territory.

So yes, writing a fantasy story in one day is wild. But it doesn't have to feel chaotic. With a clear direction, creative fuel, and ChatGPT handling the heavy lifting of names, phrases, descriptions, and ideas, you're free to focus on the part that matters most—*telling the story only you can tell.*

Creating an Ending That Feels Like Destiny

There's a unique kind of satisfaction in a fantasy ending that feels like destiny. Not just because the prophecy came true or the sword was returned to the stone—but because every step, every scar, every sacrifice led your hero to this final moment. A great ending in fantasy doesn't just wrap things up—it *resonates*. It feels inevitable, not predictable. It feels earned. When you're writing a fantasy story in a single day, crafting a satisfying ending might sound like a tall order—but with clarity, emotional honesty, and a little help from ChatGPT, you can write a conclusion that lands with weight and wonder.

The first step to writing a strong ending is knowing where you're going *from the start*. Destiny isn't about surprise—it's about **alignment**. Your ending should reflect the central idea of the story. If your tale is about sacrifice, the ending must show what was given up. If it's about rebellion, the ending must show change. If it's about love, loss, freedom, or identity, your final moments should bring those themes full circle. You can use ChatGPT to get grounded:

"What kind of ending would feel satisfying for a story about a cursed hero learning to forgive themselves?"

This gives you a target to write toward—even if you take a few scenic routes along the way.

Once you know the *feeling* you're aiming for, think about the **choices** your characters make. Destiny in fantasy isn't just about fate doing its thing—it's about people confronting fate, questioning it, defying it, or becoming it. Give your protagonist a final decision that costs something, that reveals how much they've changed, that could only be made by *this version* of them, here and now. Try prompting:

"Write a fantasy ending where the hero refuses the throne they fought to reclaim,"

or

"Describe a scene where a character embraces their destiny, even though it means becoming the thing they feared."

A powerful ending often echoes the beginning—but altered by growth. Maybe the final scene mirrors the first, but this time, the hero stands taller. The town they fled is now a place of return. The name they once denied is spoken with pride. You can use prompts like:

"Give me a final scene that reflects and reverses the opening scene of a fantasy journey,"

or

"How can I close a story where the character's belief in magic is restored after losing it?"

These connections give the story a mythic symmetry.

Emotionally, your ending should leave readers *feeling* something. It might be triumph. It might be grief. It might be bittersweet silence. The key is to make sure the emotions match the weight of what's come before. If your hero has lost everything, don't fake a happy ending. If they've found themselves, don't drown it in gloom. You can ask ChatGPT:

"What emotional tone suits the ending of a story about a reluctant hero who finds their voice?"

and it will help you zero in on how to hit the right chord.

Don't be afraid of **quiet endings**. Not every fantasy story needs to end in a battle. Sometimes, the most powerful moment is a choice not to fight. A moment of stillness. A moment where something small means everything. Like a sword laid at someone's feet. A letter finally sent. A simple line like: "The storm had passed. For now, that was enough."

Use your world's magic to make the ending *feel larger than life*, even if the moment is intimate. The forest sighs. The stars rearrange. The magic fades. The dragon bows. These are not just plot details—they're **symbols**. Ask:

"What magical signs could signal the end of an ancient curse?"

or

"Describe a quiet magical event that shows peace has returned to the realm."

These touches turn your ending from just an event into a legend.

One technique that works especially well in fantasy is the **echo of prophecy**—but twisted or fulfilled in an unexpected way. Maybe the hero was "destined to destroy the world"—and they do, only to build something better. Maybe the "savior" was never meant to be the protagonist, but someone they inspired. You can ask:

"How do I subvert a prophecy in a way that still feels true?"

Destiny doesn't have to be straightforward. But it should *click* into place.

Another trick? **Leave a thread behind.** Not every ending needs to be neat. Sometimes, the most satisfying endings hint at something still unknown. The villain's body is never found. A child hums a forgotten spell. The wind carries the voice of someone long gone. These touches give your story a sense of **continuing myth**, like the world moves on even after the page ends.

Ask ChatGPT:

"Write a final paragraph that closes a fantasy story but leaves one detail hauntingly unresolved."

This is how you leave readers thinking about your world long after they've finished the last line.

Ultimately, a fantasy ending that feels like destiny is about *truth*. Not the truth of the prophecy, or the rulebook, or the lore—but the truth of the journey. Who your hero became. What they lost. What they chose. And what it cost them to stand at the end of the road.

So whether your final scene is a coronation or a funeral pyre, a kiss or a quiet walk into the woods, make sure it *matters*. Not because it's epic—but because it's *right*.

In the next chapter, we'll explore **how to revise your one-day fantasy story quickly and effectively**, using ChatGPT to polish, strengthen, and clarify your draft without losing the creative fire that brought it to life.

Editing in the Moment: Refining Paragraphs as You Go

In a perfect world, writing and editing would be two separate stages. You'd write your fantasy story in one big creative rush, then come back later with your editor's cap on, smoothing sentences and sharpening meaning. But when you're writing a complete fantasy story in a single day, you don't always have the luxury of time. That's where **editing in the moment** becomes a survival skill—not to slow you down, but to keep the flow clean, your voice strong, and your momentum *alive*. With ChatGPT riding shotgun, you can catch clunky phrases, weak descriptions, or flat dialogue in real time—without losing your place in the story.

Editing while you write doesn't mean obsessing over every word. It means **noticing friction**—a sentence that doesn't sit right, a beat that doesn't land, a description that feels too vague—and making small, meaningful adjustments *as you go*. It's like adjusting the sail while you're still sailing. You don't drop anchor every time the wind shifts. You tweak.

So how do you make that work in fast fantasy drafting?

Start by training your eye to **spot small problems, not big ones**. You're not rewriting entire chapters. You're fixing tone, flow, and clarity. If a sentence feels long and flat, don't start over—trim it. If a line of dialogue feels stiff, loosen it. If your pacing feels sluggish, shorten a scene or punch up a sentence. ChatGPT can help with this in the moment. Try:

"Rewrite this paragraph to feel faster-paced,"

or

"Make this line of dialogue sharper and more in character."

You're not asking for a full revision—you're asking for a quick boost.

Let's say you've just written a battle scene, and it reads fine—but it doesn't *sting*. You feel like it's missing that emotional hook. You can prompt:

"Add emotional weight to this fight without making it longer,"

and ChatGPT can weave in stakes, fear, memory, or desperation with just a few word choices.

You can also use real-time editing to **enhance voice**. Every character should sound different. If you realize two of your characters are speaking in the same cadence, pause and ask:

"Rewrite this dialogue in the voice of a sarcastic rogue,"

or

"Make this sound like an ancient priestess who speaks in riddles."

Now your world gets richer without you needing to stop and study your own character sheets.

Editing in the moment also means trusting your instincts. If a paragraph makes you frown or skim—fix it *now*. Don't flag it for later if later might not come. If you write a line like "The wind howled across the plain," and it feels generic, just prompt:

"Give me a more vivid version of this sentence that fits a dark fantasy tone."

You're making quick swaps—freshening your pages without breaking stride.

Here's a great trick: when you're stuck in a sentence, don't overthink—**tag in the AI**. If your fingers freeze, type a quick note:

"[Make this moment more intense—character sees their mentor fall],"

and move on. Or better yet, let ChatGPT try it for you right there:

"Write a 2-sentence reaction from a young warrior watching their mentor get killed."

Now you're not pausing to over-analyze—you're plugging the hole and sailing forward.

You can also use ChatGPT to clean **description clutter** on the fly. Fantasy writers often overwrite—layers of adjectives, too many metaphors. If you write:

"The dark, dusky, decaying ruins loomed like the bones of forgotten gods,"

and it starts to feel purple, prompt:

"Simplify this sentence without losing atmosphere."

In seconds, you'll have a cleaner version—and more control over tone.

Don't be afraid to edit structurally mid-way, too. If you realize a scene isn't earning its place, ask:

"How can I combine this travel scene with a character reveal to keep the pace up?"

or

"What's a better way to introduce this lore without stopping the story?"

You don't need to rewrite from scratch—you just need to adjust your angle.

And let's talk about **momentum-preserving edits**—your best friend in one-day writing. These are small tweaks that make big differences. You can ask:

"Change this exposition into a short exchange between two characters,"

or

"Rework this inner monologue into something tighter and more emotional."

It keeps the draft strong without slowing your pace.

Real-time editing also helps with **repetition and redundancy**. If you catch yourself using the word "glow" five times in a chapter, highlight it, then prompt:

"Give me alternative ways to describe magical glowing effects in a fantasy world."

Now your imagery stays fresh—and your writing doesn't get stuck in loops.

One word of warning: don't let in-the-moment editing become **perfection paralysis**. If something's *good enough to move on*, move on. Drop a comment or a placeholder if you're unsure. Example:

"[This scene needs more emotional payoff—come back if time allows.]"

That's editing with strategy, not obsession.

The magic of editing as you go is that it lets you finish your story *without creating a mountain of rewrites later*. You're solving problems at the source. And with ChatGPT guiding your hand, it's like writing with a second pair of eyes—one that doesn't sleep, doubt, or lose track of the stakes.

So stay light on your feet. Keep typing. Fix what needs fixing in real time. And trust that polishing a sentence while the story's hot in your head is often more effective than waiting until the fire's gone cold.

Making the Magic Matter: Thematic Resonance in Fantasy

Fantasy is full of spell-books, prophecies, glowing runes, and enchanted weapons—but none of it truly matters unless it means something. That's where **thematic resonance** comes in. It's what happens when your story's magic does more than move the plot—it *mirrors the message*. When a curse reflects guilt, when a healing spell tests forgiveness, when a magical journey becomes a spiritual awakening. The most unforgettable fantasy stories don't just entertain—they echo with meaning. And when you're writing a fantasy tale in a single day, threading your magic to your theme gives your story a sense of cohesion, purpose, and emotional power that sticks with the reader long after the final page.

To begin with, you don't need a big theme spelled out like a thesis. You just need a guiding idea—something your story is *about* beyond the surface action. That might be freedom, grief, power, identity, redemption, fear, faith, or love. Once you know the emotional or philosophical undercurrent of your story, you can shape the magic to reflect it.

Start by asking ChatGPT:

"What kind of magic system reflects a theme of personal sacrifice?"

or

"Describe a form of magic that embodies the idea of emotional repression."

You'll get responses that not only inspire worldbuilding, but tie directly into the character journeys and conflicts your story will explore.

For example, if your theme is **control versus freedom**, maybe magic in your world is accessed only through obedience to ancient laws—and your protagonist breaks those rules to find a deeper, wilder power. If your theme is **grief**, perhaps magic is drawn from memory, and the more one remembers, the more potent—but also the more painful—it becomes. You can prompt:

"Give me a magic system based on remembering the dead,"

or

"What kind of magical consequence fits a story about losing faith in tradition?"

When magic reflects your theme, every spell becomes symbolic. A sword that can only be drawn when you forgive yourself. A spell that reveals truth but hurts the one casting it. An enchantment that binds people in love, but dissolves the moment doubt creeps in. These aren't just cool mechanics—they're **emotional storytelling tools**. Ask ChatGPT:

"Suggest magical objects that reveal hidden truths at a personal cost,"

or

"Design an enchanted forest that changes shape based on the traveler's fear."

Magic can also serve as a **lens for character growth**. If your hero begins the story afraid of change, their magic might initially fail until they embrace the unknown. If your character is arrogant, their power might seem limitless—until they're forced to give it up to save someone. ChatGPT can help you connect arc and ability:

"Describe a magic system where power fades as the character grows more selfless,"

or

"What magical trial could symbolize the shedding of an old identity?"

Villains, too, can be shaped thematically through their use of magic. If your story explores the danger of unchecked ambition, maybe the antagonist uses a form of magic that burns the world around them the more they draw on it. If the theme is deception, their power might manipulate memory or truth. You can ask:

"Create a villain who uses illusion magic to hide their own vulnerability,"

or

"What kind of curse would a character use to control others under the guise of protection?"

Don't forget that **magical rules can embody philosophical or moral ideas**. In *Fullmetal Alchemist*, equivalent exchange isn't just a mechanic—it's the story's central ethical principle. In *The Name of the Wind*, naming is power because names reveal truth. Think about what your story believes, and let the magic agree, argue, or evolve alongside it. You can prompt:

"What's a magic system where balance must be maintained at all costs?"

or

"Invent a magical tradition built around the idea that emotion is the purest form of power."

You can also use magic as a **mirror of society**. If your theme explores inequality, maybe only a certain bloodline can access magic—or perhaps magic is abundant, but hoarded by the elite. Ask ChatGPT:

"Describe a society where magic is taxed and regulated, and how rebels subvert it,"

or

"What kind of magical discrimination could reflect a theme of social division?"

And then there's the **personal symbolism** of magic. What spell does your hero use most? What object do they carry? What power scares them? These choices can say more about who they are than dialogue ever could. A warrior who carries a healing charm. A mage who refuses to learn a spell that killed someone they loved. Use prompts like:

"What kind of magic item could represent a character's inner guilt?"

or

"Describe a spell that only works when cast with full sincerity."

Finally, use your **climax** to tie it all together. The final magical act—whether it's casting a spell, breaking a curse, sacrificing power, or refusing to use it at all—should reflect the theme at its peak. If your story was about identity, the hero's final act should declare who they really are. If it was about love, it should test or affirm that love. Ask:

"Write a fantasy climax where the hero's sacrifice proves they've learned the story's lesson,"

or

"Design an ending where the use of magic resolves both plot and personal arc."

When the magic matches the message, your story gains resonance. You're not just saying, "Look at this cool spell." You're saying, "This spell *means* something." It's not just enchantment—it's *emotional logic*. And even in a single day, even in a short piece, you can hit that note.

So make the magic matter. Let it reflect, enhance, and challenge your story's theme. Let it be more than a mechanic. Let it be metaphor. That's how fantasy becomes more than escapism—it becomes myth.

Generating Perspectives

One of the most important decisions you'll make when writing your fantasy story—especially in a single day—is **point of view**. It's the lens through which your reader experiences the world, the voice in their ear, the consciousness that filters every sword fight, whispered prophecy, and impossible choice. Whether you choose first-person, third-person limited, or omniscient point of view, each offers its own strengths, weaknesses, and storytelling flavor. Picking the right one helps you write faster, stay grounded, and tell your fantasy tale with clarity and emotion.

Let's start with **first-person**. This is the most intimate point of view—you're right inside the character's head. Everything the reader knows, sees, or understands is filtered through the "I." First-person is great for stories with strong emotional arcs, unreliable narrators, or internal conflict. When the hero is discovering the world as the reader is, first-person can heighten tension, immersion, and connection.

A first-person voice lets you lean into personality. A brooding assassin will sound very different from an excitable apprentice mage. You can use ChatGPT to experiment with tone:

"Write a first-person passage from a thief sneaking through a noble's garden while hiding a stolen spell-book."

You'll get voice, perspective, and emotion in one.

But first-person also comes with limits. You can't easily switch between characters. You can't show scenes happening elsewhere unless your protagonist is witnessing them. That's why first-person works best in stories where the protagonist is central to every key event. If you're writing a tight, emotional, character-driven fantasy in a single day, first-person can give you momentum by locking you into a single perspective from the start.

Next, there's **third-person limited**—one of the most common and versatile POVs in fantasy. It uses "he" or "she," but still follows one character closely, giving you access to their thoughts, perceptions, and emotions without being as subjective as first-person. It gives you breathing room: you can describe things more cinematically, while still keeping the reader emotionally connected to your hero.

Third-person limited is ideal for stories where you want some narrative distance—maybe to show the world in more detail or build tension outside of your character's awareness, but still stay grounded in their journey. It also lets you shift perspectives between scenes if needed. For instance, you could follow the hero in one chapter, then jump to the villain's POV in the next to increase dramatic irony. ChatGPT can help you structure this:

"Write a third-person limited scene where a young mage fails a trial but hides their shame."

You still get interiority—but with more flexibility.

Then there's **third-person omniscient**—the god-view. You're outside of everyone, able to dip into anyone's mind, describe scenes your hero doesn't witness, and narrate with a broader, sometimes more philosophical tone. This can give your story a grand, mythic feel. Think of a narrator who speaks like they've seen a thousand stories before and will see a thousand more.

Omniscient POV is great for stories with sweeping scope, big themes, and multiple characters whose fates intertwine. You can use it to build contrast between perspectives, drop dramatic foreshadowing, or deliver narration with flair. Try a prompt like:

"Write an omniscient paragraph showing how a kingdom reacts to the return of a long-lost heir."

You'll get a wide-angle view of emotion, geography, and culture in one pass.

But be careful. Omniscient can slip into confusion if you head-hop too quickly or if the narrator's voice isn't strong enough to carry the transitions. In a fast-writing sprint, omniscient is best used when you've planned how it flows—or when you want your story to feel more like folklore or legend than personal journey.

So how do you choose the right POV for your story?

Ask yourself:

- **How personal is the story?** If it's all about the internal transformation of one character, first-person or third-person limited will serve you better.
- **Do you want to explore more than one mind?** If yes, third-person limited with shifting POVs—or omniscient—gives you that room.
- **What tone are you going for?** First-person is immediate. Third-person limited is balanced. Omniscient is grand and reflective.
- **How much does the reader need to know beyond what the character knows?** If your plot depends on irony, hidden plans, or dramatic turns the hero can't see coming, third-person or omniscient can handle it better than first-person.

You can even combine styles. A story might begin with an omniscient prologue, then dive into third-person limited for the main narrative. Or you could use first-person journal entries between third-person scenes. Just ask ChatGPT:

"How can I mix POV styles in a fantasy story without confusing the reader?"

It'll help you experiment without losing clarity.

Ultimately, the best point of view is the one that **helps you tell the story the way it feels in your head**. Don't choose what's trendy—choose what gives you momentum and emotional truth. And if you're still unsure? Write your opening scene in a few different POVs and see what flows. ChatGPT can generate each version in seconds, letting you compare and choose without second-guessing.

What a Scene Looks Like in a Fantasy Screenplay

So you've built a magical world, shaped your hero's journey, crafted a plot full of war, wonder, and dragons—and now you want to see it on screen. Transitioning from a fantasy novel to a screenplay might feel like a leap across a chasm filled with smoke and winged beasts, but it's actually a matter of learning how to think visually, economically, and structurally. Screenwriting is about *what we see and hear*—not what characters feel inside unless that feeling is expressed through action or dialogue. And in fantasy, it's your job to make the impossible feel inevitable and cinematic.

Let's break down what a **scene** in a fantasy screenplay looks like—and how to write one quickly, clearly, and creatively.

Every screenplay scene starts with a **slugline** (also called a scene heading). This tells us where and when the scene takes place.

It looks like this:

EXT. MISTWOOD FOREST – NIGHT

That line says we're outside (EXT.), in a place called Mistwood Forest, and it's nighttime. If your scene happens inside, you'd use INT. (for interior). If it transitions between places (like inside a cave that opens to the sea), you can say something like:

INT. CAVE MOUTH – DUSK – CONTINUOUS

You don't need to describe every blade of grass or magical rune in the slugline. That comes next.

Below the slugline, you write **scene description**—short, punchy paragraphs that describe what the viewer sees and hears. In fantasy, this is where you create atmosphere fast. Think visual. Think sound. Think movement.

Example:

Fog coils around twisted roots. A distant howl echoes through the trees.

A cloaked figure pushes through the undergrowth—limping, bleeding, clutching a satchel that pulses with pale green light.

In just two lines, you've painted a mood and set up a mystery. You didn't say what the character feels—but we feel it through the image and motion.

Now for **character introduction**. The first time a character appears, you write their name in ALL CAPS with a quick, visual description:

The figure lowers their hood. This is LYRIA (17), wild-eyed, with soot-streaked cheeks and a fire in her stare.

Don't overload with adjectives. Just give us the vibe. In a fantasy world, you want the reader to see who this person is immediately—whether it's a warrior in bloodied armor or a noble with emerald sigils sewn into silk.

Then comes **dialogue**, formatted like this:

LYRIA

The relic... it's not just waking the old gods.

VOICE (O.S.)

(cold, amused)

You always were slow to understand prophecy.

Note a few things here:

- Character names are centered and capitalized.
- Dialogue is beneath the name.
- You can use **parentheticals** (like "panting") to show how a line is said—but don't overuse them.
- O.S. means "off screen"—someone is speaking, but not visible yet. You can also use V.O. for "voice over."

Fantasy dialogue can be poetic, cryptic, or dramatic—but it still needs to sound real in the moment. Keep it sharp. Give it rhythm. Try prompts like:

"Write fantasy dialogue between a dying knight and the apprentice they failed."

or

"Rewrite this fantasy monologue to be more subtle but still mystical."

When you want action or movement to interrupt, use **clear line breaks**:

Lyria draws a blade from her boot—curved like a crescent moon.

The forest falls silent. Even the wind forgets to blow.

A shadow passes overhead. She looks up—

This pacing gives your fantasy scene room to breathe. You're directing emotion through rhythm.

And remember: **screenplay scenes are short**. If your scene drags on, cut to a new location or time. This keeps your fantasy world dynamic. For example:

EXT. BLACK SPIRE CITADEL – DAWN

Crows scatter from the ramparts as the gates swing open.

INT. BLACK SPIRE CITADEL – THRONE ROOM – MOMENTS LATER

King Theron (60s, regal and tired) sits hunched on a jagged throne of obsidian.

THERON

(softly, to himself)

Let the gods decide. I am done deciding.

Just like that, you've moved from sweeping exterior to emotional interior with a few lines.

You can also use **montages** for travel, magic training, or battle buildup:

MONTAGE – THE RISING OF THE REBELLION

– Blacksmiths forge blades with glowing runes.

– Secret symbols are painted on city walls.

– Lyria stands on a cliff, raising her blade to a stormy sky.

Montages let you show big shifts quickly without overloading your page count.

Lastly, remember that in a screenplay, **what isn't said matters as much as what is**. Reactions. Pauses. Glances. Magic in fantasy isn't just in spells—it's in subtext. You can prompt ChatGPT with:

"Write a fantasy scene where two lovers say goodbye without using the word 'goodbye.'"

or

"Describe a moment of magical realization using only visuals and sound."

These scenes hit hard—and they're pure cinema.

So what does a fantasy screenplay scene look like?

It looks *tight, visual, active,* and *emotionally charged.* It's not about internal thoughts—it's about *showing everything through action, expression, and dialogue.* With ChatGPT to help brainstorm, rephrase, or block scenes, you can write a fantasy screenplay that moves fast and feels rich, even on a deadline.

Turning a Story Idea into a Series with AI

So you've got a killer fantasy story—maybe a one-day masterpiece or a short novel powered by dragons, curses, and betrayal. But when you reach the end, you realize something... this world isn't done. The characters still have arcs to grow through. The villain's plan isn't fully unraveled. The magic system hints at deeper truths. In other words: you're not writing a one-off anymore. You're writing a **series**. And with the help of ChatGPT, turning your single idea into a multi-book or multi-episode fantasy epic doesn't just become possible—it becomes *efficient*, *flexible*, and wildly *fun*.

The first step is simple: step back. Look at your original story idea and ask:

What's the larger world this tale hints at?

Often, your first story only explores one kingdom, one character arc, or one piece of magic. Use ChatGPT to help brainstorm the broader picture:

"What deeper conflict might exist behind a story about a cursed forest and a missing heir?"

or

"How can a story about recovering a relic become part of a larger series arc about the return of ancient gods?"

You'll start seeing possibilities unfold—prequels, sequels, spinoffs, character-driven side plots.

Next, think about **structure**. Will this be a trilogy? A five-book saga? A limited TV miniseries with six episodes? Ask ChatGPT to help shape that decision:

"Suggest a five-book arc based on a fantasy story where magic is returning to a world that once outlawed it."

You'll receive a skeleton outline of how each installment can escalate stakes, deepen themes, and introduce new layers of conflict.

Your goal is to find the **core thread** that ties the whole series together. Maybe it's a prophecy. A war. A magical transformation that changes the world across time. Use prompts like:

"What could be the central mystery driving a seven-part fantasy series?"

or

"Give me a long-term goal for a protagonist who begins their journey as a reluctant hero."

From there, build out your **character arcs over time**. Your protagonist can't just beat bigger bosses in every book. They need to *grow*, fail, question their values, and evolve. Ask ChatGPT:

"What stages of emotional growth might a character go through in a fantasy series about confronting their lineage?"

You can map out turning points for books 1, 3, and 5, giving you strong anchors for pacing and payoff.

Use the same process for your **antagonists**. Maybe your villain dies in Book 2—only for a worse force to rise. Or maybe the original villain becomes an uneasy ally. You can brainstorm:

"What multi-book arc could I create for a villain who begins as a tyrant but slowly loses their grip on power?"

Series work best when **each entry has its own complete arc**, while still feeding into the larger plot. Think of each book or episode like a puzzle piece: satisfying on its own, but part of a greater design. Ask:

"Give me a summary of book 2 in a fantasy series that continues the rebellion while introducing a new magical threat."

Now comes the fun part—**expanding your world**. A series gives you room to explore cultures, religions, histories, rival kingdoms, or long-lost lands that didn't fit in the original story. Ask:

"What locations could be introduced in the second and third books of a fantasy saga about a broken empire?"

World expansion deepens your setting and keeps your readers or viewers eager to see what's next.

AI is also brilliant at helping you **track continuity**. Use it to keep character histories, political systems, and magical rules consistent across entries. You can create quick lore checks with:

"Summarize the rules of dream magic established in book one,"

or

"List all the times the relic was used before book four."

This saves you from rereading everything during development—and helps keep your story universe believable.

And don't forget about **recurring motifs or themes**. These are the emotional glue of a series. Maybe each book deals with a different fear. Maybe the seasons change to reflect character growth. Maybe a line from the first chapter echoes in the final scene of book seven. Ask:

"Suggest a recurring symbol for a fantasy series about memory and time,"

or

"How can I tie each book's title to the larger series theme of transformation?"

Finally, if you ever feel like your idea isn't "big enough" for a series, ask ChatGPT to help you *scale up*. Even a small, personal story can become a series when expanded the right way. Try:

"How can I expand a single-day journey into a multi-part fantasy series?"

You'll discover that stories have layers you never knew were there—until you ask.

So don't be afraid to dream bigger. That one-off fantasy tale you wrote on a whim? It might be the first thread in a sprawling tapestry of conflict, love, betrayal, and legacy. With ChatGPT as your co-author and world architect, you're not just extending a story—you're building a *saga*.

How to Prompt for a Chapter That Writes Itself

Every writer dreams of that magical moment when the words just *flow*. The characters move, the dialogue sings, and the world builds itself like you're watching it happen instead of forcing it into place. When you're writing a fantasy story in one day, these moments are golden—and with the right approach to prompting, you can *engineer* them. This chapter is about learning how to prompt ChatGPT in a way that gives you a chapter so rich, so specific, and so alive that it practically writes itself. It's not just about asking for a scene. It's about asking *cleverly, clearly, and creatively*.

The secret to a self-writing chapter lies in **specificity plus momentum**. You don't want a vague "write a fantasy chapter about a battle." That'll give you something—but it won't be emotionally connected, character-driven, or thematically relevant. Instead, give your prompt shape and purpose. Something like:

"Write a fantasy chapter where the protagonist is forced to duel their former mentor in a ruined temple while a storm rages outside. The fight should be emotional, not just physical, and should reveal the mentor's secret."

Now you've got setting, characters, emotional stakes, and a twist. With that kind of setup, the chapter doesn't just write—it *unfolds*.

Let's break down what makes an ideal prompt for a self-writing chapter:

1. Set the Stage

Tell the AI where the scene takes place. Fantasy thrives on environment—enchanted forests, ancient halls, floating cities. When you give your scene a visual setting, it immediately gives the AI room to breathe with descriptive magic.

Prompt idea: *"Describe a chapter set in a floating marketplace where time passes differently."*

This allows the AI to generate setting, culture, tension, and maybe even magical consequences without needing to be told twice.

2. Identify the Emotional Core

A chapter with no emotional throughline might look good—but it won't *feel* good. Make your prompt personal. Who's hurting? Who's changing? What's at stake emotionally, not just physically?

Try: *"Write a chapter where the protagonist must choose between saving their love interest or retrieving the artifact that could end the war."*

Now the story has weight. Every line will revolve around that core dilemma.

3. Introduce Conflict or Discovery

Great chapters pivot. Something must be gained, lost, revealed, or risked. So include that in the prompt. Ask for a turning point, a reveal, a decision, or a danger.

Prompt examples: *"Write a chapter where the hero discovers the villain is their half-sibling."*

"Create a scene where the main character realizes their magic is slowly killing them."

These don't just keep the plot moving—they build character and deepen the world.

4. Keep Dialogue in Play

Ask for scenes that aren't just action—but *interaction*. Conversations, arguments, confessions—these make chapters breathe. They show how your characters relate to each other and evolve.

Prompt idea: *"Write a dialogue-heavy chapter where the hero and their rival are trapped together in a crumbling tomb and are forced to talk while waiting for rescue."*

It'll generate not only suspense but deepening relationships.

5. Use Genre Language

Remind the AI what kind of fantasy you're writing. Is it high fantasy? Dark fantasy? Romantic fantasy? Urban? Mythic? The tone shifts dramatically based on genre cues. A "gritty low-magic fantasy world" reads very differently than "an ethereal dreamlike realm governed by moon spirits."

Prompt examples: *"Write a mythic fantasy chapter about a character walking through the land of forgotten gods."*

"Create a dark fantasy chapter set in a city where magic must be hidden or punished."

6. Give It a Goal

Finally, tell ChatGPT what the chapter should *do*. Advance the plot? Reveal a secret? Foreshadow doom? Having a story objective keeps the AI focused.

Example: *"Write a chapter where the protagonist finally earns the trust of their companion by sharing the truth about their past."*

This prompt gives an emotional target and lets the chapter write itself toward that goal.

If you want to generate variations or options, you can always prompt: *"Give me three different versions of this chapter—one focused on emotion, one on action, and one on mystery."*

Now you can pick the one that feels most right—or blend them into a layered draft.

You can also use follow-up prompts to revise as you go: *"Rewrite this to make the stakes more urgent."*

"Add a metaphor using the forest to reflect the character's fear."

"Give this chapter a stronger final sentence."

These micro-edits shape the raw output into something polished without stopping your forward momentum.

And if you're starting from scratch, try this all-in-one master prompt:

"Write a 1000-word chapter in a dark fantasy story. The protagonist, a reluctant sorcerer, must rescue a cursed child from an abandoned temple. The temple shifts shape with emotion. The chapter should build tension, deepen the sorcerer's inner conflict about using their power, and end with a haunting discovery about the origin of the curse."

That's how you make a chapter *write itself*—by giving the AI just enough fuel, direction, and pressure to generate something you can shape into gold.

Using Flashbacks, Dreams, and Visions to Deepen the Story

In fantasy, time doesn't always have to move forward. Sometimes the most powerful truths lie in the past, or hidden deep in the mind, or delivered from beyond by firelit dreams and half-seen gods. Flashbacks, dreams, and visions are more than just stylistic tools—they're storytelling devices that let you show character history, world lore, emotional wounds, and foreshadowing without stopping the story's pace. Used wisely, they deepen everything. They create echoes across your story. They let readers glimpse the unseen—and when you're writing fast, they allow you to drop whole lifetimes into just a few paragraphs.

Let's break each one down and explore how to use them creatively and efficiently with help from ChatGPT.

Flashbacks: Revealing the Hidden Past

Flashbacks are like memory keys. They unlock who a character *really* is by showing us what made them that way. In fantasy, this might mean a traumatic spell gone wrong, a childhood betrayal, a lost love who still haunts them, or a lesson from a mentor now gone. The best flashbacks aren't random—they're **triggered**. Something in the present makes the past resurface.

You can prompt ChatGPT like this: *"Write a flashback where the hero remembers the first time they used forbidden magic—and why they swore never to do it again."*

Flashbacks work best when they:

- Reveal **why** a character fears, hates, or hides something.
- Echo the emotional stakes of the current moment.
- Provide vital **context** for decisions being made now.

Keep them short and focused. A flashback isn't a detour—it's a **reveal**. Drop it in like a blade, twist, and return to the present.

Ask ChatGPT to help with: *"Write a 300-word flashback that explains why the protagonist never enters temples."*

Or go deeper: *"How can I weave flashbacks into a story without breaking the momentum?"*

You'll get techniques like embedding memories inside action or dialogue—like a character seeing a broken sword and remembering who wielded it last.

Dreams: Emotional Mirrors and Hidden Messages

Dreams in fantasy are rich territory. They can be purely symbolic, deeply emotional, or genuinely magical. In a dream, your character can confront their guilt, see their destiny, or relive a moment they've buried. Dreams can offer **emotional honesty**—because there's no pretending in a dream.

Dreams also offer **visual power**. They're surreal, strange, and full of symbolism. A mother turning to ash. A child walking backward through snow. A city underwater, glowing with forgotten language. These images hit harder than exposition ever could.

Use prompts like: *"Describe a dream sequence where the protagonist is hunted by versions of themselves."*

"Write a dream that warns the hero of an approaching betrayal without naming the traitor."

Let ChatGPT help you turn inner turmoil into dreamlike narrative. You can even ask: *"Give me dream symbolism for a character who fears becoming like their father."*

The key with dream scenes is to make them **emotional first, meaningful second**. Don't just plant clues—create *feeling*. The best dream sequences don't explain everything. They hint, disturb, provoke.

Visions: Magic, Prophecy, and Destiny

Visions are a staple of epic fantasy. They can be magical—sent by gods, spirits, or the land itself—or mystical, a result of bloodlines, prophecy, or a bond with something ancient. Visions can be clear or cryptic, terrifying or beautiful. But like flashbacks and dreams, they should serve a purpose: to **warn**, to **guide**, or to **reveal**.

Unlike dreams, visions often come with a cost. Maybe they age the seer. Maybe they bleed into reality. Maybe they can't be trusted. Ask ChatGPT to help raise the stakes: *"What price could a seer pay every time they receive a vision?"*

Or: *"Write a vision that seems like hope but turns out to be a curse."*

Visions work well at turning points in the story:

- When the hero is doubting their path.
- Before a major battle.
- Just after a tragic loss.
- When magic is spiraling out of control.

Prompt ChatGPT with: *"Write a vision of the future shown to a character who swore never to wield magic again."*

Or: *"Create a vision sequence that uses surreal imagery to foreshadow the villain's rise."*

Visions often carry **symbolic layers**. You can ask: *"What visual symbols could represent a collapsing kingdom?"*

"How might a vision foreshadow a friend's betrayal using weather or animals?"

Let AI help you pack your visions with thematic resonance.

Weaving Them Seamlessly into Your Story

Flashbacks, dreams, and visions aren't chapters you bolt onto the story—they're **threads woven into it**. You can use them:

- Between action scenes to build depth.
- At night while characters rest, reflecting what's just happened.
- During a ritual, magical accident, or near-death experience.
- Triggered by an object, location, or piece of music.

Ask ChatGPT: *"What are natural moments for a character to experience a memory while traveling through a familiar place?"*

Or: *"Write a transition from a dream into waking reality that shows the character shaken but changed."*

Used well, these scenes can:

- Fill in character backstory *without exposition*.
- Foreshadow future events or twists.
- Connect readers to emotions your character won't speak aloud.
- Add mystery and complexity to the pacing of your story.

Even in a single-day draft, you can slip in these scenes with precision. Let ChatGPT help you write them quickly, clearly, and beautifully—then return to the present with more weight, more emotion, and more story to tell.

Creating Fantasy Titles That Grab Attention

A great fantasy title doesn't just label your story—it casts a spell. It promises wonder, danger, mystery, or myth before a single page is turned. It can conjure entire worlds in just a few words. And when you're writing a fantasy novel or short story in a single day, crafting the perfect title might seem like an afterthought—but it's actually one of your most powerful tools. The right title grabs attention, teases your tone, and hints at your core themes. With help from ChatGPT, you can generate title ideas that are not only memorable but perfectly matched to the heart of your story.

Let's start by looking at what makes a fantasy title *work*. Whether it's **epic and sweeping** like *The Name of the Wind*, **mysterious and haunting** like *A Song of Ice and Fire*, or **action-driven** like *The Way of Kings*, the best fantasy titles tend to do one or more of the following:

- Hint at the **world or mythology**
- Tease a **central conflict, object, or prophecy**
- Name a **key character, creature, or group**
- Evoke a strong **tone**—romantic, tragic, epic, dark, mysterious
- Use poetic or evocative **language** (names, verbs, metaphors)

So how do you find your own?

You start by prompting smart.

Try this with ChatGPT: *"Give me 10 fantasy book title ideas based on a story about a cursed heir who must reclaim a broken kingdom from within."*

You'll get results like:

- *The Crown Beneath Ashes*
- *The Broken Throne*
- *Oath of the Forgotten Blood*
- *The Curse of the Hollow Heir*

You can then refine further: *"Make the titles more mysterious,"* or *"Add a romantic or tragic tone."*

Let's break it down further by category, so you can prompt for exactly what kind of title you're after.

1. Titles Based on Character

If your story centers around a singular, iconic character, you can use their title, role, or mythic status to build the name.

Examples:

- *The Last Oracle*
- *Daughter of the Storm*
- *The Witch and the Warden*
- *He Who Burns the Sky*

Prompt ideas: *"Give me fantasy titles centered on a fallen knight seeking redemption."*

2. Titles Based on Place

Sometimes, your setting *is* the story. If your world is unique or if your plot revolves around a cursed land, a forbidden city, or a mystical forest, use the place as the hook.

Examples:

- *The Shores of Athelwen*
- *Beneath Hollowspire*
- *The Gates of Elira*
- *Empire of the Drowned*

Prompt ideas: *"List fantasy titles based on a city that was swallowed by magic."*

"Give me haunting names for a ruined magical kingdom."

3. Titles Based on Objects or Magic

If your story revolves around a magical artifact, spell, or system, focus on the object itself—especially if it carries mystery or power.

Examples:

- *The Ember Codex*
- *The Blade That Whispers*
- *A Curse for Every Crown*
- *The Mirror of Memory*

Prompt ideas: *"Give me fantasy titles based on a magical book that corrupts its reader."*

or

"What are poetic titles for a story about an enchanted sword that chooses its wielder?"

4. Titles Based on Themes or Symbolism

Some fantasy titles lean more abstract or symbolic, especially when the story is about destiny, time, grief, or transformation.

Examples:

- *A Requiem of Stars*
- *We Who Wait in Silence*
- *Threads of Fire*
- *To Wake the Gods*

Prompt ideas: *"List fantasy titles that evoke themes of loss and rebirth."*

or

"What are some lyrical fantasy titles about forbidden love and forgotten magic?"

5. Title Formats That Just Work

You can use reliable formats as templates:

- **The [Adjective] [Noun]**
  The Silent Blade, The Crimson Pact, The Shattered Throne
- **[Noun] of [Noun]**
  Daughter of Flame, Tears of the Moon, Lord of Chains
- **[Verb] the [Noun]**
  Kill the Warden, Summon the Night, Break the Sigil
- **[Character] and the [Noun]**
  Elira and the Nine Keys, Ashen and the Serpent Crown

Ask ChatGPT: *"Give me fantasy titles using the structure '[Noun] of [Noun]' for a story about a soul-bound warrior."*

or

"Suggest titles with verbs like 'Break,' 'Summon,' or 'Bind' for an action fantasy."

You can even take your actual story beats and use them as inspiration. For example, if your story is about a sorceress who dies and is resurrected in a ruined temple by forgotten gods, prompt:

"Suggest titles for a fantasy story about a resurrected sorceress seeking revenge in a temple of dead gods."

You'll get options like:

- *Ash and Divinity*
- *The Sorceress Who Returned*
- *Gods of the Hollow Temple*
- *Her Magic, Undone*

And if you want something *totally new*, use blending prompts like: *"Combine romantic fantasy and cosmic horror into ten title ideas."*

This way, your fantasy title isn't just a label—it's the *first line of the story*, the mood setter, the promise.

Finally, don't be afraid to **test variations**:

- Add or remove an article (*Thorn vs. The Thorn*)
- Swap one word to shift tone (*The Blood Pact* vs. *The Crimson Pact*)
- Use made-up or mythic words sparingly (*The Mourning of Yelthar* works if the name has weight)

In the end, the title you choose should **spark curiosity**, fit the tone of your world, and—most importantly—*feel like part of the legend.*

Pulling the Reader Through with Cliffhangers and Curiosity

In fantasy, the world might be vast, the magic epic, and the characters unforgettable—but none of that matters if the reader doesn't want to turn the page. What keeps someone reading isn't just spectacle—it's **suspense**. It's the itch of an unanswered question, the shadow of a choice not yet made, the footstep heard just before the chapter ends. If you want your fantasy story to move fast and feel irresistible—even when you're writing it in a single day—you need to master the art of cliffhangers and curiosity. These tools pull readers through your tale like a current, from opening line to final page.

Let's start with the obvious: a **cliffhanger** doesn't have to mean someone dangling off a literal cliff. It just means the chapter ends at a point where something is *about to happen*—and the reader *has* to know what.

Here's what great cliffhangers look like:

- A door creaks open—but we don't see who's behind it.
- A character hears their name whispered in a dead language.
- A sword is drawn, and the page ends before the strike lands.
- A character says, "There's something I need to tell you..." and the scene cuts.

Each of these is a promise. It says, "Come with me to the next page—I'm not done yet."

You can ask ChatGPT: *"Give me five fantasy cliffhanger endings for a chapter involving a forbidden spell."*

or

"What's a suspenseful last line for a scene where the hero enters the villain's sanctum?"

These last lines are critical. They should crackle with urgency, mystery, or danger. Try:

- *And then, the lights went out.*
- *She smiled like someone who knew exactly how the world would end.*
- *The map burned in his hands, but the mark on his skin still glowed.*

But here's the twist: not *every* chapter needs a cliffhanger. Sometimes, you hook the reader not with danger—but with **curiosity**.

Curiosity lives in questions. The reader sees a symbol they don't understand. A prophecy with a missing line. A character who flinches at the name of a place—and we don't yet know why. It's not just "What happens next?" It's *Why is this happening at all?* It's the pull of an unsolved riddle, a truth buried under silence.

Ask ChatGPT: *"Give me mysterious details to reveal in a chapter that make readers curious about a forgotten war."*

or

"What's a subtle clue that something's wrong with the hero's bloodline?"

Curiosity builds *tension* over time. Maybe you don't explain the villain's motive until book two. Maybe the old king's ring has a sigil no one recognizes—and it's never commented on again... until the final act.

One of the best ways to build curiosity is through **character reactions**. When someone reacts to something *we* don't yet understand, it hooks us. For example:

- A soldier sees a scar on the prince's back—and goes silent.
- A seer hears a child's name and drops their cup.
- A beast refuses to enter the temple, even though it's never been afraid before.

You can prompt: *"What are ten character reactions that hint at a deeper mystery in a fantasy story?"*

And then you let that mystery simmer. The reader will follow you, waiting for the answer.

Another technique? Use **delayed consequences**. Something strange happens—but the fallout comes later. A character casts a spell that seems to work—but the air smells wrong. A relic is claimed—but the sky darkens hours afterward. Let ChatGPT help you layer the suspense: *"Describe a fantasy scene where magic appears to work perfectly—but one character notices something is subtly wrong."*

That's how you build a chapter that pulls instead of pushes.

If you're writing a fantasy series or longer story, plant **multi-chapter hooks** too. A vision that hasn't come true. A name we keep hearing but haven't met. A character who's obviously lying—but we don't know why.

And for short stories or one-day books, use **chapter endings** as stepping stones. Each should pose a question, offer a choice, or change the status quo.

Ask: *"What's a dramatic way to end a chapter after a failed magical ritual?"*

or

"Write the final line of a chapter where two characters realize they've misjudged the villain."

Here are a few formats that work:

- **Reversals:** Everything we believed is now wrong.
- **Reveals:** A new truth just came to light.
- **Decisions:** The hero has to choose—but we don't see the outcome.
- **Threats:** Something dangerous is coming—and we feel it.
- **Interruptions:** A quiet moment is shattered.

You can even generate a batch with: *"Give me ten types of fantasy chapter cliffhangers across different emotional tones—fear, awe, betrayal, mystery."*

With this toolbox, your fantasy story becomes a series of promises. Not just "What will happen?" but "What *does it mean*?" "Why is this important?" "How far will they go?"

That's how you write chapters readers can't walk away from. That's how you write fast *and* keep them turning pages.

How to Write a Twist That Feels Like Fate

The best plot twists in fantasy don't come out of nowhere. They feel *earned.* They feel inevitable in hindsight, but impossible to guess in the moment. They land not because they shock—but because they *reveal.* A great twist doesn't rewrite the story—it reframes it. Suddenly, everything the reader thought they knew was true... still is, but not in the way they believed. And when a twist feels like fate—when it ties into the world, the theme, and the character's emotional journey—it stops being just a surprise. It becomes a legend.

In fantasy, you've got a powerful advantage: a world filled with magic, prophecy, bloodlines, curses, and forgotten truths. All of these are natural homes for twists. But if you're writing fast—like in a one-day draft—you need to build your twist *into* the foundation. With the help of ChatGPT, you can structure your twist in a way that's efficient, poetic, and devastatingly effective.

Let's start with what makes a twist *feel like fate.*

It begins with **foreshadowing**. Not in bold letters—but in little echoes. A twist that hits hard has *roots.* Maybe it's a line of dialogue that felt casual. A strange look. A moment the hero can't quite explain. Later, it all makes sense.

Ask ChatGPT: *"Give me subtle ways to foreshadow that the villain is actually the hero's brother."*

or

"How do I hint at a magical object being cursed without revealing it too soon?"

When the twist comes, the reader doesn't feel tricked. They feel awakened.

A twist also needs **reversal**. Something the reader (and hero) believed must flip. The hero trusted the king—but the king is the traitor. The spell meant to save the world was the key to ending it. The chosen one is the villain's child. These twists strike because they don't change the truth—they *deepen* it.

Prompt idea: *"Write a twist where the character fulfills the prophecy—but not in the way anyone expected."*

This kind of twist feels like fate because the story has been *moving toward it* all along—just in a direction you didn't see.

Use twists to also expose **character truth**. The strongest ones aren't about shocking the reader—they're about showing who your hero really is.

For example:

- A coward sacrifices everything.
- A noble betrays their cause to protect someone they love.
- A character who swore never to kill... does.

Ask: *"What kind of twist reveals a character's deepest fear to be their greatest strength?"*

or

"How do I structure a twist that redefines the hero's identity without rewriting their arc?"

Another tool: use **symbolism and recurring imagery** to tie the twist to the theme. Maybe the hero keeps dreaming of drowning—and in the twist, we learn they were drowned and reborn as a child. Maybe the land has always reacted to them, and now we discover *they* are the source of the imbalance. Now the twist isn't just a fact—it's the heart of the myth.

Ask ChatGPT: *"Give me symbolic elements that could foreshadow a twist about a character being unknowingly immortal."*

You can even reverse expectations **in your magic system**. Maybe the price of magic isn't life—it's memory. Maybe the ancient enemy isn't real—it's a creation of the ruling class to keep the people united. These changes work best when the audience assumed one thing because *everyone* in the story did.

Prompt: *"Describe a twist that turns a magical belief system inside out without undermining the world's logic."*

It's also helpful to ask: *"What twist could make the reader reinterpret the entire first half of the story?"*

These are the moments that feel mythic. They don't just advance the plot—they reveal that the story was always leading here.

Here are a few types of twists that often feel like fate in fantasy:

- **The Identity Twist**: The hero is the child of the enemy, or the reincarnation of a lost god.
- **The Prophecy Twist**: The chosen one is misunderstood—or deliberately misled.
- **The Magic Twist**: The hero's power is not a gift—it's a curse or a burden passed down.
- **The Loyalty Twist**: The mentor was protecting the villain—or the villain was protecting the hero.
- **The Cause Twist**: The rebellion is fighting the wrong war. The ancient enemy was misunderstood.

Each of these gains power when tied to **personal stakes**. The twist should matter to the plot—but more importantly, it should *break or transform* the protagonist.

A few guiding questions you can ask ChatGPT during your twist creation:

- *"What is something the hero believes that, if proven false, would change everything?"*
- *"How can I make a twist feel tragic but also inevitable?"*
- *"What is a poetic way to reveal that a character's greatest strength has always been their greatest danger?"*

Finally, when writing the twist scene, let the **emotion lead**. Don't just drop facts. Let the character *react*. Let the world shift around them. If they realize they were the villain's weapon all along, show the weight of it—the silence, the denial, the rage, the crumbling of certainty. That's what makes it land.

Prompt: *"Write the scene where the protagonist learns the truth about their origin—and that it means they can never return home."*

Let it feel like loss. Or freedom. Or the moment destiny closes its grip.

A twist that feels like fate isn't just a turn in the plot—it's the moment the *truth is revealed*. And once it's out, nothing can be the same.

Using Your Own Voice While Working with AI

When you sit down to write a fantasy story in a single day with the help of AI, one question might start tapping at the edge of your mind: *Is this still me?* The fear is natural. You're not just typing words alone—you're co-creating. But here's the truth: using ChatGPT doesn't erase your voice. It *amplifies* it. It's a tool, not a ghost-writer. And the more you work with it, the more your voice comes through—not despite the AI, but because you're choosing what to ask, what to shape, what to keep, and what to rewrite.

Your **voice** isn't just how you describe a sword or a forest. It's how you feel about the story you're telling. It's the kind of pain you let your hero feel. It's your rhythm, your themes, your taste in metaphors. Whether you write in a lyrical tone or a punchy one, whether your stories are full of dry humor or tragic undertones—that *is* you. And ChatGPT doesn't take that away. It listens. It mimics when asked. And it offers ideas, not replacements.

Let's explore how to stay grounded in your unique storytelling style, even while leaning on AI to speed things up, explore possibilities, or fill in the blanks.

Start with **the way you prompt**. The more you personalize your questions, the more you inject your voice into the response. For example:

Instead of asking:

"Write a fantasy scene where a hero defeats a monster."

Say:

"Write a tense, character-driven scene where the hero kills a monster not with strength but with empathy—and regrets it afterward."

Now you're not just asking for a scene. You're asking for *your kind* of scene. The way you frame the request tells the AI what *matters to you* as a storyteller.

You can even go a step further: *"Write this in a tone that's bittersweet, with short sentences and poetic rhythm—less Tolkien, more Le Guin."*

Or: *"Rewrite this scene using language that feels ancient but clear—no modern slang, no sarcasm."*

ChatGPT listens. It adapts. But it doesn't decide what tone to strike—you do. And once you've trained it with your preferences, it starts becoming a much better creative partner.

One way to reinforce your voice is to **use AI for structure, not soul**. Let it help you map the beats of a chapter, design a city, brainstorm side characters. Then, when you write or revise, bring your own flair to the dialogue, to the emotion, to the metaphors. Ask for ingredients—but cook it your way.

Try this split:

- Ask ChatGPT: *"Give me a list of emotional beats for a scene where a hero returns to the village they abandoned."*
- Then write the scene yourself in your voice, or ask: *"Help me rewrite this scene with a melancholy tone and one moment of dry humor."*

You don't need to accept the AI's first draft. You can reshape it, expand it, or stitch it to your own text. If a phrase feels off, change it. If a paragraph sings, use it. If the AI uses a cliché you'd never write, prompt:

"Rewrite this paragraph in a style that avoids fantasy clichés and uses more original language."

Your **editing choices** are also part of your voice. Even if the AI suggests twenty ideas, the one you choose is the one *you* felt. That's authorship.

You can also train the AI over time by saying: *"This is a sample of my writing style. Please try to match the tone in the next chapter."*

Paste a paragraph of your own. Show it what "your voice" sounds like. Then say:

"Now write the next scene in this same style, keeping sentence length, tone, and imagery consistent."

This turns AI into a mirror. Not a replacement—but a reflection that helps you keep the voice strong across your story.

And here's something else: **your voice grows by reacting.** You might see a line ChatGPT suggests and think, *No, that's not right—this is how I'd say it.* That *moment*—that decision—is your voice getting sharper. You're not becoming reliant on AI. You're becoming *clearer about what you want.*

And that clarity is power.

It's okay if you copy and paste a paragraph that feels "perfect" right out of the AI. You made the prompt. You made the decisions. You sparked the idea. That makes it yours. You're the conductor, not the passenger.

As you work faster, and write more, and finish stories you used to only dream of finishing, you'll start to hear your voice more loudly in every word—*because* of this process, not in spite of it.

So go ahead. Use AI for ideas. For speed. For finding the perfect title or building a city in five seconds. But remember: *you* are the one shaping the story. The choices are yours. The heart is yours. And the voice that echoes in your reader's mind—that's not the voice of an algorithm.

It's the voice of a writer who used magic as a tool, not a crutch.

The Value of Archetypes in Fantasy Storytelling

Fantasy storytelling is full of echoes—shadows of ancient myths, old wisdoms wrapped in new worlds, and characters that feel both fresh and deeply familiar. That's not a coincidence. That's the power of **archetypes**. They're not clichés. They're the **core patterns** we've always told stories around. The orphan hero. The wise mentor. The trickster, the tyrant, the chosen one. These figures exist because they speak to something elemental inside us. They're blueprints that transcend time, culture, and geography. And when you use them well—especially with help from ChatGPT—they can supercharge your fantasy story with emotional weight, clarity, and mythic resonance.

Archetypes work because they connect to universal truths. But they're also flexible. You're not locked into writing a cookie-cutter farm boy who becomes a warrior king. You can twist the archetype, modernize it, gender-flip it, give it flaws, stretch it sideways. The trick is to **start with the archetype**, then personalize it. That's where ChatGPT becomes your storytelling ally.

Let's break down a few classic fantasy archetypes and how to use them creatively:

The Hero

The Hero's archetype is about transformation. It's Frodo leaving the Shire. It's Aragon becoming king. It's someone who starts unsure and becomes what they were always meant to be. You can prompt ChatGPT like:

"Give me five variations of a reluctant hero archetype with unique backstories."

or

"How can I make a hero who refuses the call but still ends up saving the world?"

Your hero doesn't need to be noble or powerful at the start. They just need a reason to grow—and something worth risking everything for.

The Mentor

This is the character who guides the hero, usually carrying wisdom, regret, and maybe a hidden past. Think Gandalf, Merlin, or Moiraine. But you can twist the role:

- What if the mentor is wrong?
- What if they're using the hero?
- What if they die early—and their teachings weren't what they seemed?

Ask: *"Describe a mentor figure in a fantasy story who teaches through riddles and illusions—and may not exist at all."*

Suddenly, the archetype becomes an enigma.

The Villain

The Villain isn't just evil—they're the **shadow** of the hero. A fallen version. A mirror. They're what the hero could become if they chose differently. You can make them tragic, charming, or even sympathetic. Ask:

"Create a fantasy villain who was once a healer but turned to dark magic after losing everything."

or

"How can I build a villain who believes they're the real hero of the story?"

The more layered the villain, the more powerful their presence.

The Trickster

Often the comic relief, the wildcard, or the disruptor of the status quo. Think Loki, Puck, or the thief who steals more than gold. Tricksters are fantastic for shaking up structure, injecting energy, or delivering harsh truths with a grin. You can ask ChatGPT:

"Give me fantasy trickster characters who also carry deep emotional scars."

or

"Write a scene where the trickster saves the day—but no one realizes it."

They're unpredictable—and that makes them gold for pacing and tension.

The Threshold Guardian

This archetype shows up when the hero needs to grow to continue. It might be a literal gatekeeper, a rival, or even a flaw within themselves. They aren't evil—they're **a test**. You can prompt:

"Create a threshold guardian who challenges the hero's identity, not their strength."

This can lead to some of your most meaningful character moments.

The Shapeshifter

This character is unstable—maybe literally, like a changeling or skin-walker, or emotionally. They change allegiance. They lie. They surprise. Think of them as the tension knife in your cast. Ask:

"Give me a fantasy shapeshifter who falls in love with someone who knows their secret."

Shapeshifters keep your reader guessing—and questioning what's true.

The Herald

This character calls the hero to action. They might deliver a prophecy, a warning, or a vision. Sometimes they vanish afterward. Or maybe they're part of the long game. Ask:

"Describe a mysterious herald who brings a message but speaks only in broken dreams."

The Herald doesn't need to be a character—it can also be a storm, a corpse, a birthmark. Anything that tells the hero: *You're not who you think you are.*

Now, why are archetypes so valuable when working with AI?

Because they give you **structure fast**. You can say: *"Give me a story outline with a hero, mentor, trickster, and shapeshifter. Make the trickster the real villain."*

And just like that, you've got bones to build on.

You can layer archetypes, too:

- A mentor who becomes the villain.
- A hero who starts as a threshold guardian for someone else.
- A villain who is also a herald for a greater evil.

Ask: *"How can I combine archetypes to create a more complex character?"*

ChatGPT will give you combinations that create natural conflict and surprise.

Archetypes also help with **theme**. A story about sacrifice might include a hero, a martyr, and a betrayer. A story about identity might revolve around a shapeshifter, a false mentor, and a hero in disguise. You can prompt:

"Which archetypes best support a fantasy theme of freedom vs. control?"

That's how you build not just a plot—but *a myth.*

And if you ever worry about sounding too familiar? Twist it. Flip it. Break it and rebuild it. Archetypes are tools, not rules. With the right prompt, you can make them brand new:

"Give me a fantasy story where the villain follows the Hero's Journey—and wins."

That's how you create archetypes that don't just echo old stories—they *become* new legends.

Writing Across Cultures without Falling Into Stereotypes

Fantasy has always been about other worlds—lands with different rules, different languages, different ways of life. So it's only natural for writers to reach across cultures for inspiration when building their own realms. But there's a line between creating a rich, respectful fantasy world inspired by real cultural ideas, and falling into shallow stereotypes or accidental caricature. The good news is that when you're writing fast with AI—and especially when you're writing fantasy—you have the chance to be both *creative* and *careful* at the same time.

The key to writing across cultures with respect is to focus not on imitation, but on **interpretation and invention**. You're not recreating someone's lived experience—you're building something *inspired* by the textures, values, aesthetics, philosophies, and storytelling traditions of real-world cultures. The fantasy genre gives you the freedom to remix—but with that freedom comes the responsibility to treat those roots with care.

So how do you build fantasy cultures that feel diverse, authentic, and layered—without sliding into cliché?

Start with Humanity, Not Exoticism

People are people. Whether your character is from a desert empire inspired by North African history or a mountain city reminiscent of Tibetan culture, their beliefs, fears, rituals, and dreams should make emotional sense. Don't let your curiosity turn into objectification.

Instead of asking: *"What do shamans wear in jungle cultures?"*

Try: *"What role might a spiritual healer play in a fantasy society that believes dreams predict war?"*

That shift focuses on **function and belief**, not visual stereotype.

With ChatGPT, you can ask: *"Help me create a fantasy culture with storytelling traditions inspired by oral histories, not written texts. What might their legends sound like?"*

This leads to deeper worldbuilding that's respectful, creative, and unique.

Avoid One-Note Cultures

One of the biggest traps in fantasy is the "monoculture"—where every person in a certain place dresses the same, thinks the same, and speaks the same. Real cultures are **complex, messy, contradictory**. They evolve. They clash internally. There are radicals, traditionalists, mystics, skeptics, urban dwellers, rural wanderers, merchants, priests, rebels, scholars—all with different values.

Ask ChatGPT to help you layer this: *"Describe internal factions within a fantasy desert kingdom. Include political, spiritual, and generational divides."*

Suddenly, your "inspired-by" culture has richness and realism.

Use Names and Language Thoughtfully

It's tempting to mash consonants together and call it worldbuilding. But names carry history, sound, and tone. If you're drawing inspiration from a real language or culture, be careful not to appropriate words that hold sacred or painful meaning in the real world. Avoid random borrowing that sounds "foreign."

Instead of: *"Give me fantasy names that sound Asian,"*

Ask: *"Create a fantasy naming convention based on a culture that uses nature, seasons, and birth order to name children."*

Now you're thinking like a linguist and a storyteller—not a collector of tropes.

Be Aware of Power Dynamics

Fantasy is filled with kings, empires, conquerors, and rebels. When writing across cultures, especially if you're from a dominant or privileged background, be mindful of how power operates in your story. Are you unintentionally framing a foreign-inspired people as primitive? As magical but inferior? As a backdrop for the hero's journey?

Ask ChatGPT to check your assumptions: *"Does this story setup risk repeating a colonial narrative? How can I avoid that?"*

This kind of self-check doesn't kill creativity—it **deepens it**. It helps you build better stories with fewer blind spots.

Don't Just Borrow Aesthetic—Engage with Meaning

It's easy to grab the surface of a culture: clothes, temples, food. But what do those things *mean* in context? Why is a ritual done at dawn? Why are certain colors sacred? Why is a festival held on a mountain?

Ask: *"What kind of seasonal festival might exist in a fantasy world where light is seen as a fragile gift?"*

Now your culture grows from the **inside out**, not from a Pinterest board of "exotic inspiration."

Use Multiple Lenses

Every culture includes internal tension. Don't just show it from the outside—let people from within your fictional world **disagree** about their own beliefs. Let them argue over tradition. Let them see their own rituals differently based on age, class, or personal experience.

Ask ChatGPT: *"Give me two characters from the same culture who view their ancestral magic very differently—one reveres it, one resents it."*

This not only avoids stereotype—it creates *story*.

Invite Feedback and Stay Curious

Even in a fast-draft process, you can pause to check yourself. If your fantasy culture draws inspiration from real traditions—especially if those cultures have faced oppression or misrepresentation—consider asking ChatGPT: *"Does this portrayal risk reinforcing a stereotype? How could I explore this idea with more care?"*

Or prompt it to offer alternatives: *"Instead of a jungle full of 'savages,' what's a more respectful and interesting setup for a reclusive forest civilization?"*

These revisions are small but powerful.

Your voice matters. And when you draw from a wide world of ideas, histories, and philosophies, your fantasy stories become more expansive, more vibrant, and more meaningful. But it's your responsibility to use that inspiration with sensitivity—not because you're afraid to write, but because you *care* enough to write with heart and respect.

Writing across cultures isn't about walking on eggshells. It's about walking with awareness—and seeing other ways of life not as strange or mystical or decorative, but as deeply human.

How to Make Your Fantasy Feel Ancient and New

One of the greatest powers of fantasy is its ability to feel timeless. The best fantasy stories seem like they were whispered through the ages—passed down in firelight, carved into cave walls, sung under stars. And yet, those same stories feel alive and urgent, full of characters and conflicts that speak directly to today. That's the sweet spot: a story that feels **ancient and new** at the same time. If you can tap into that balance—even in a single-day draft—you create something that resonates like myth and moves like a modern epic. The secret? It's all in the way you *layer your storytelling.*

Let's talk about how to build fantasy that carries the weight of history and the pulse of the present—with the help of ChatGPT to speed the process and deepen your world.

Start with Echoes, Then Twist Them

Fantasy feels ancient when it draws on the shapes of old stories—archetypes, cycles, prophecies, curses, bloodlines, fallen empires. These elements whisper of a deeper past. But if you stop at familiarity, you fall into cliché. The trick is to **echo something timeless**—then bend it into something unexpected.

Ask ChatGPT: *"Give me a twist on the 'chosen one' trope where the prophecy was mistranslated."*

or

"Invent a magical item that was revered in the past but is now feared."

Now you're honoring the old while inventing the new.

Build a World With Ruins, Relics, and Remembering

Ancient-feeling fantasy worlds aren't shiny. They're layered. They have lost languages, crumbling cities, broken statues, forgotten gods. Even if you don't explain every bit of lore, suggesting depth gives your story the feeling that it extends *before page one.*

Try prompts like: *"Describe a city built on the bones of a forgotten civilization, with remnants woven into everyday life."*

"Give me cultural traditions passed down for centuries, whose original meanings are now lost."

A character lighting candles because they always have—without knowing why—feels more mythic than one reciting a full history lesson.

Use Language That Carries Weight

The way you phrase things can make them feel eternal. Choose language that has rhythm, that feels spoken aloud, that sounds like it's been repeated. Use metaphors that evoke nature, time, or death. Lean into gravity—but sparingly. And then pair that weight with modern pacing, character intimacy, and emotional honesty to keep the story feeling fresh.

Ask ChatGPT: *"Rewrite this paragraph with a more mythic tone—use poetic rhythm, ancient-sounding imagery, and symbolic language."*

Or try: *"Write a line of prophecy that sounds old and ominous but carries a modern emotional punch."*

Mixing the lyrical with the raw keeps your fantasy grounded and mystical.

Play With Time in the Plot

A great way to create contrast between the ancient and the new is to let your story deal with **time itself**. Maybe your characters awaken something old. Maybe the world is recovering from a forgotten age of gods. Maybe the hero is part of a cycle that has happened before—this time, with a twist.

Use prompts like: *"Write a scene where a character realizes they're repeating a choice made by a long-dead ancestor."*

"Describe a place where time folds, and the past bleeds into the present."

Suddenly, your story becomes a dialogue between now and then.

Let the Past Haunt the Present

Fantasy that feels ancient has a past that *won't stay buried*. Ghosts, magical scars, songs that carry warnings. The idea that the world remembers, even if the people don't. This gives your story atmosphere, tension, and poetry.

Ask: *"What are magical consequences of breaking an ancient treaty long forgotten by mortals?"*

"Give me a myth told to children that turns out to be literal in a new context."

When your characters live in the aftermath of something older than they understand, everything feels bigger.

Keep the Characters Real

The best contrast comes when you pair the mythic with the **relatable**. An ancient setting with modern emotions. A prophecy-bound warrior with anxiety. A goddess of war who wants to grow a garden. When characters feel human, even in a world of relics and ruins, the reader stays emotionally grounded.

Prompt: *"Describe a scene where a character fulfills an ancient rite but struggles with imposter syndrome."*

This gives your story heat and heart—keeping the fire of the old world burning in new ways.

Invent New Myths and Legends

You don't need to borrow from real-world folklore to build something timeless. Use ChatGPT to generate your own internal mythology:

"Create a legend about the creation of the moon in a fantasy world where magic is tied to tides."

or

"What is a bedtime story told to children in a world where dragons are extinct?"

These small details give your world memory—and memory is the essence of age.

The key to making fantasy feel ancient and new isn't about copying what's come before. It's about **respecting pattern while breathing life into it**. You're not retelling myths. You're *writing new ones*. And with the power of fast, intentional prompting, you can do it on the fly. In hours. In one day. With emotion, clarity, and voice.

Because when your world feels like it's always existed—and your story feels like it was meant to be told *now*—you're not just writing fantasy. You're writing legend.

Finishing the Draft by Midnight: Pacing Your Writing Day

You've got your idea, your world is spinning with magic and mystery, your characters are ready to rise or fall, and the sun is barely peeking over the horizon. It's go time. The challenge? You've got one day—*just one*—to write your entire fantasy story. Maybe it's a novel. Maybe it's a tight short story or a screenplay. Whatever the format, the clock is ticking, and the finish line is midnight. But here's the good news: with the right pacing, a smart rhythm, and ChatGPT as your writing partner, you can absolutely do this—and do it well.

Writing fast isn't about racing. It's about **flow**. It's about knowing where your energy goes, when to push, when to pause, and how to keep momentum alive without burning out. In this chapter, we'll build a realistic plan to get you across the finish line with a full draft in hand and maybe even time to spare.

Start with a Morning Launch Pad (8:00 AM – 10:00 AM)

The first two hours are sacred. You're fresh, you're not overloaded with caffeine or stress, and your imagination is still half-dreaming. This is the best time to *establish your foundation.*

What to do:

- Use ChatGPT to generate your story summary, chapter outline, or screenplay beats.
- Lock in your characters: name, archetype, arc, and motivation.
- Set up your world: magic system, setting, and tone.

Prompt example: *"Give me a 10-chapter outline for a fantasy story about a healer who discovers they're the reincarnation of a tyrant king."*

By 10 AM, you want to have a roadmap. Not perfect. Not detailed. Just enough to keep you writing instead of wondering.

The First Big Writing Block (10:00 AM – 1:00 PM)

This is where you start **writing chapters** or **scenes**. You're riding that early momentum. You're not overthinking.

Your goal: 3,000 to 5,000 words by lunch. That's enough to get you deep into Act 1 and set things in motion.

Tips:

- Use ChatGPT to generate first drafts of scenes you're unsure about.
- When stuck, ask for the next beat:
  "What's the next logical event after the hero discovers the map was forged?"
- Let AI handle small things—descriptions, names, transitions—so you can stay in the zone.

Midday Momentum Reset (1:00 PM – 2:00 PM)

Take a break. Walk. Stretch. Eat. Don't stare at your screen. Don't read what you've written. Just reset.

Then do a micro-check-in:

- Where are you in the outline?
- Is the story still emotionally on track?
- Are you avoiding filler and moving toward the core conflict?

If you're behind, no panic. Ask ChatGPT: *"How can I combine the next two story beats into one fast-paced chapter?"*

The Heart of the Story (2:00 PM – 6:00 PM)

This is your **Act II engine room**. Conflict rises. Stakes grow. Twists arrive.

Use this time to:

- Hit your story's midpoint reversal.
- Deepen character arcs.
- Introduce your twist, magical turning point, or betrayal.

Your word goal here is 4,000 to 6,000 words. But more importantly, you're climbing the hill toward the final act.

Use ChatGPT to write supporting scenes fast: *"Write a dialogue between the hero and villain that reveals a shared past."*

Or: *"Describe a magical trial that tests the hero's deepest fear."*

Stay emotionally connected to your characters. Even in speed writing, heart matters more than polish.

The Evening Push (6:00 PM – 9:00 PM)

You're tired—but now you know the end is near. This is **Act III**. Everything you've set up now pays off.

Your goals here:

- Bring relationships to a head.
- Resolve the main arc.
- Write your emotional climax.
- Hit the theme that ties everything together.

Ask ChatGPT: *"Write a final battle that's more emotional than physical."*

or

"Give me an ending scene where the hero walks away from the crown they've won."

You don't have to finish beautifully. You just have to *finish clearly*.

Final Lap (9:00 PM – 11:30 PM)

Now it's clean-up and closing. This is where you:

- Write or refine your epilogue.
- Scan for dropped plot threads.
- Reconnect opening and closing beats.
- Add connective tissue if any scenes feel thin.

Ask: *"What's a poetic way to echo the opening scene in the final paragraph?"*

or

"Give me a closing line that leaves a haunting question unanswered."

If you have 30–45 minutes left before midnight, you can even ask ChatGPT: *"Summarize this story into a blurb."*

or

"Give me five title ideas that reflect the emotional arc."

Now you're polishing the surface of something solid.

What If You Run Out of Time?

If you don't finish everything, don't stress. Use ChatGPT to help summarize or flesh out what's left.

Prompt: *"I need to wrap this story up in one final scene—here's what's unresolved. Help me close it quickly but satisfyingly."*

You'll still walk away with a complete draft. That's more than most writers accomplish in a week.

At the end of the day, finishing your draft by midnight is not about perfection—it's about momentum. It's about rhythm and decision and not letting doubt slow you down. It's about staying in motion. And with ChatGPT by your side, you don't have to stop to overthink. You can prompt for pacing, ideas, transitions, or emotion whenever you need a boost.

So get up early. Write with fire. Pivot when stuck. And keep going until you write those final words—*even if they come with ten seconds left on the clock.*

Using ChatGPT to Polish Prose and Fix Awkward Phrases

So you've done it—you've written your fantasy story in a single day. Your characters faced monsters, fulfilled prophecies, and maybe even saved (or doomed) the world. But now, as you glance back at the draft, you spot it. That awkward phrase. That clunky line of dialogue. That paragraph that felt okay at 3 p.m. but reads like it was written during a lightning storm at midnight. Welcome to the polishing phase.

Luckily, you've got a secret weapon: ChatGPT. When used well, AI can help you clean up your prose *fast*, without losing your voice, tone, or momentum. It's not just about grammar—it's about **refining the rhythm of your story**, smoothing the jagged edges, and turning raw narrative into something that reads like you actually meant every word all along.

Here's how to do it.

Start by Identifying What Feels Off

You don't need to rewrite everything. Focus on what makes you hesitate as you read:

- Sentences that sound robotic or overlong
- Descriptions that don't land
- Dialogue that feels wooden or forced
- Repetition of the same phrase or idea
- A metaphor that doesn't quite make sense

Highlight those moments. They're not failures—they're just **unfinished thoughts**.

Now you can prompt ChatGPT with laser focus: *"Rewrite this paragraph to make it more vivid and emotionally engaging:"*

and paste your section.

Or: *"This dialogue feels stiff. Make it more natural and give it subtle tension."*

You're not erasing your voice—you're **amplifying it** through smarter phrasing.

Match Tone and Style

You can tell ChatGPT exactly what tone you're aiming for. Maybe you want something lyrical, something gritty, or something archaic. Be specific.

Prompt examples:

- *"Rewrite this scene with a tone like Tolkien: poetic and formal."*
- *"Make this paragraph sound darker, with more tension and sensory detail."*
- *"Polish this description of a magical forest so it feels dreamlike but eerie."*

This lets you keep full control over your stylistic identity—while letting ChatGPT handle the fine-tuning.

Work With Sentences, Not Just Whole Scenes

You don't have to send in full scenes. Try working sentence by sentence when you hit trouble. Something like:

Original:

"The dragon was big, with eyes like burning coals and wings that flapped loudly."

Prompt:

"Rewrite this sentence to be more vivid and poetic, while keeping the description clear."

ChatGPT might return:

"The dragon loomed, its coal-red eyes glowing with ancient fire, wings slicing the sky with thunderous grace."

You can take that, adjust it further, or blend it with your original to make it yours. It's collaboration, not replacement.

Fixing Repetition and Sentence Flow

A common issue in speed writing is **repetitive sentence structure**. Too many "He did this. Then he did that. She looked. He turned." It makes even exciting scenes feel flat. You can fix this with:

"Vary the sentence structure in this paragraph while keeping the same meaning."

Or: *"Remove repetitive phrasing and improve sentence rhythm here."*

ChatGPT will smooth things out while respecting your content. It's like a rhythm check in real time.

Sharpening Dialogue

Fantasy dialogue often drifts into one of two extremes: *too modern* or *too stiff*. Use ChatGPT to balance tone and character voice:

"Rewrite this dialogue to feel more natural while keeping a formal medieval tone."

or

"Make this argument between a rogue and a noble sharper and more emotional."

The AI can help you shape each character's voice distinctively while keeping the tension alive.

Punching Up Passive Phrasing

Fast writing often leans on passive language. You can fix it in a flash:

"Rewrite this paragraph to eliminate passive voice and make the action more direct."

Or: *"Make this battle description more active and immediate."*

These tweaks keep your prose energized—and that matters when you're editing on a deadline.

Add Polish, Not Padding

You don't want your cleaned-up story to become overwritten. Tell ChatGPT:

"Polish this paragraph without making it longer."

or

"Make this more elegant, but keep the word count close to the same."

You'll get tighter, cleaner prose that doesn't lose its pacing or power.

You Can Even Get Line-Level Feedback

If you're feeling really stuck on something, go granular:

"What's awkward about this sentence, and how can I rewrite it to be smoother?"

Or even: *"This line is okay, but I want it to land with more emotional impact. Suggestions?"*

This kind of feedback loop helps you improve—not just this draft, but your own instincts as a writer.

In the end, polishing with ChatGPT isn't about handing over your work for rewriting. It's about **having a tireless, objective assistant** who can spot what you missed, rephrase what you're unsure of, and offer suggestions on demand. You still decide what stays. You still shape the voice. You are the writer. ChatGPT is the sharpening stone.

So go through your draft with curiosity. Highlight anything that catches your eye. Then let AI offer new angles, clearer phrasing, or poetic upgrades. Don't fear the awkward line—fix it in seconds and keep moving forward.

Testing the Logic of Your Magic System with AI

Every great fantasy story needs rules—especially when it comes to magic. It's tempting to treat magic like a get-out-of-jail-free card, a tool to escape any tight plot corner or make anything possible. But readers know when it's too convenient. They sense when it's inconsistent. And nothing breaks immersion faster than a spell that works perfectly one moment and fails for no reason the next. That's why a **logical magic system** is so important—and why ChatGPT can be your secret spell checker when it comes to making sure your magic makes sense.

Let's walk through how to build, test, and refine a magic system that feels rich, balanced, and narratively satisfying—without spending weeks writing rulebooks. AI is here to help you stress test the rules and spot loopholes before your readers do.

Start With a Clear Premise

Before you can test a system, you need to define it. Magic doesn't need to be fully scientific, but it needs **boundaries**, **costs**, and **consistency**. Begin by prompting:

"Help me define a magic system where spells are powered by emotion, but the stronger the feeling, the more damage it does to the caster."

Or: *"Design a magic system based on written contracts with nature spirits. Each spell is a deal."*

Once you have the core idea, you can move into world-specific logic.

Ask "What If" Questions to Stress-Test the System

This is where ChatGPT becomes a diagnostic tool. Feed it your system and ask:

"What are the potential loopholes in this magic system?"

"How could someone abuse or exploit this system?"

"What would happen if two people used this magic in conflicting ways?"

"If this power existed, how would it affect politics, trade, or daily life?"

These prompts help you see beyond the flashy spells and into the consequences—the ripple effect of your system across society, warfare, religion, even romance.

You can also test narrative tension: *"What limits can I add to this system to make it more challenging for the hero?"*

"How can this magic fail at the worst possible moment, but still make sense?"

These questions not only make your story stronger—they make your world feel alive.

Use ChatGPT to Build Magic-Specific Conflict

If your magic system is all reward and no risk, it becomes boring fast. Ask:

"Create a magical duel using a system where spells are cast through singing—but the longer the song, the more power it gains."

or

"Write a scene where two mages use elemental magic, but each is bound by strict environmental limits."

This helps you visualize your magic system under pressure—and see whether the rules hold up.

You can also prompt: *"Design a trial or magical test that challenges someone to use their magic creatively under restriction."*

Now you're building plot and system logic at the same time.

Check for Internal Consistency

Magic needs to follow its own rules, even if those rules are strange. If your character can fly using fire magic in chapter 3, why do they hike through the mountains in chapter 12?

Paste a few rules into ChatGPT and ask: *"Do these magical rules stay consistent across the story beats?"*

"Does this character's use of magic contradict anything introduced earlier?"

Let AI point out anything that feels shaky. It won't rewrite your system—it'll flag the holes.

You can even ask: *"How might a clever character solve this problem using only the rules of this magic system?"*

Now you're not just testing logic—you're finding creative narrative solutions.

Build Exceptions That Deepen the World

Every good system has exceptions—but they must feel earned. The key is to make sure your exceptions add depth, not confusion.

Ask ChatGPT: *"What is a rare or forbidden use of this magic that was outlawed centuries ago?"*

"Describe a magical loophole that only a few know about, and why it's dangerous."

These make your system feel more like a living tradition, with history, controversy, and mystery baked in.

Add Cultural and Practical Impact

A logical magic system isn't just about combat or cool powers—it should change how people live.

Use prompts like: *"What kind of jobs would exist in a society where time magic can slow aging?"*

"How would medicine work if healing magic came with memory loss?"

"What laws or taboos might evolve in a culture where telepathy is common?"

This makes your system not just consistent—but immersive.

Ask AI to Summarize Your Magic System for Clarity

Once you've built and tested your system, ask: *"Summarize this magic system in three clear rules."*

or

"Explain this magic system in a paragraph that could go in the front of a fantasy novel."

This keeps your thinking clean. If you can't explain it clearly, your reader won't follow it either.

You can also try: *"Summarize this system in-character, as if a cynical magic tutor were teaching a student who doesn't care."*

That gives you tone, lore, and logic all in one.

A logical magic system doesn't mean rigid or boring. It means **meaningful**. When magic has rules, risks, and a rich inner logic, every time a character uses it becomes a *choice*. And when it fails—or surprises—it feels like part of a living world, not just author convenience.

ChatGPT helps you speed up that testing, uncover possibilities you hadn't considered, and tighten your system without getting lost in the weeds. So before your characters sling another spell, take the time to ask:

Does this magic make sense?

Does it challenge my characters?

Does it shape my world?

If it does, you've built something that feels real—even if it defies the laws of physics.

Checking for Plot Holes and Weak Character Arcs

You've reached the end of your fantasy draft—magic has been cast, fates fulfilled, and the final chapter is typed. But before you call it done, there's one more critical task: **making sure the bones of your story actually hold together**. Plot holes and weak character arcs are two of the most common—and most damaging—flaws in fast-written fantasy. The good news is you don't have to do this alone. With the right prompts and a little patience, ChatGPT can help you scan your story like a narrative surgeon, finding cracks in the structure before your readers do.

Let's walk through how to check for both plot holes and character arc issues efficiently—without losing the magic of your story.

Start with a Bird's Eye Summary

Before diving into details, give ChatGPT a short version of your story: *"Here's a quick summary of my fantasy novel. Can you identify any major logic gaps or inconsistencies?"*

Paste a 300–500 word overview of the plot. You'll often get useful questions in return:

- Why didn't the villain use this power earlier?
- How did the hero survive that fall without explanation?
- Why would this ally betray them out of nowhere?

Sometimes, just **retelling your story aloud** makes problems obvious. But AI can help surface what your own brain is glossing over.

Test Cause and Effect

A plot hole often comes down to a broken chain of logic. One event is supposed to lead to another—but something feels skipped, forced, or too convenient.

Ask: *"Does this plot progression make logical sense, or are there missing links between cause and effect?"*

"Does the climax resolve the central conflict using previously established tools, or does it feel like a deus ex machina?"

You can also copy-paste key turning points and say: *"Tell me if this scene contradicts anything that came before."*

Let AI help you catch the continuity errors before your readers do.

Check for Unresolved Threads

In a one-day draft, it's easy to forget the smaller things: the mentor's secret, the locked door, the mysterious vision from Chapter 3. If you drop these, readers will notice.

Prompt: *"Here's a list of the questions and mysteries introduced in my story. Can you tell me which ones were resolved and which ones weren't?"*

Or ask: *"Does the ending resolve all the major threads set up in the first act?"*

If you find loose ends that *should* stay mysterious (for a sequel or worldbuilding depth), great—just be intentional.

Character Arcs: From Flat to Full Circle

A weak character arc is when the hero either doesn't change, or changes in a way that feels unearned or unclear. Ask ChatGPT: *"Here's my main character's journey from start to finish. Does this show real internal growth, or does it feel flat?"*

You can also be more specific: *"Does this character's decision to forgive the villain feel justified based on their earlier behavior?"*

If you get feedback like "this moment feels rushed" or "the motivation isn't clear," it's a sign to go deeper—not necessarily rewrite everything, but **clarify the transformation**.

Use this checklist with ChatGPT:

- Who is the character at the beginning?
- What do they believe?
- What changes them?
- What do they believe at the end?
- What did they *choose* to do differently?

This is the emotional spine of your story. If it's intact, the whole narrative feels stronger.

Side Characters and Arcs That Disappear

In a fast draft, supporting characters sometimes show up strong—then fade. That's okay, but if you introduce a character as important, they need to contribute all the way through.

Prompt: *"Are there any supporting characters who seem important but then vanish without a payoff?"*

You can follow up with: *"How can I tie this character back into the climax without rewriting the whole structure?"*

AI can suggest elegant re-entries or small scene tweaks to make side characters feel integrated.

Check for Contradictions

One scene says the magic system requires silence. Another shows the hero shouting a spell. That's a contradiction. So is a character who hates bloodshed leading a massacre with no internal conflict.

Prompt: *"Scan this excerpt for contradictions between the world rules and character behavior."*

Or paste two scenes and ask: *"Does this later scene logically follow from this earlier one, or is something missing?"*

You can also ask: *"Does the villain's plan make sense from their point of view?"*

This checks for plot holes wrapped in character motivation.

Ask for a Reader's Perspective

Sometimes, the best test is to take off your writer's hat. Ask: *"Pretend you're a fantasy reader who just finished this story. What questions would you still have?"*

Or: *"Give me feedback on this story's consistency, pacing, and character development like an editor would."*

You'll often get a blend of technical suggestions and emotional responses. Use both.

At the end of the day, plot holes and weak arcs are not signs of failure. They're signs of *speed*. You wrote fast, you built fast, and now it's time to reinforce the structure.

With ChatGPT, you can review your work with clarity. It won't rewrite your vision—it will help you make sure that vision *holds up*. Every scene, every spell, every choice.

So take a breath. Go back through. Ask questions. Challenge your story. Patch what needs patching. Strengthen what's already working.

Creating a Fantasy Story That Feels Real

Fantasy is built on the unreal—magic, monsters, mythic quests—but the most powerful fantasy stories feel more *real* than the world outside your window. They move us, haunt us, stay with us because they reflect something deeper than dragons or enchanted swords. They capture truths about fear, hope, love, sacrifice, freedom, and fate. No matter how wild your world is, your story can resonate with honesty. And when you write a fantasy story that feels real, readers believe in the impossible—because they believe in the people at the heart of it.

In a one-day draft, it's easy to lean into spectacle and skip the grounding. That's where ChatGPT can help you balance wonder with realism, fantasy with feeling. Here's how to infuse your world with authenticity and emotional weight—fast, effectively, and without sacrificing imagination.

Ground Magic in Meaning

Start by making your magic **matter**. Not just mechanically—emotionally. Magic should have a cost, a consequence, a culture. Ask:

"What are the emotional risks of using magic that draws on memory?"

or

"Describe a society where magic is considered sacred, and misusing it is like blasphemy."

Now your world has rules, but also values. Belief systems. Conflicts of the heart, not just of power.

Real-feeling fantasy starts with internal logic and cultural depth. You don't need an encyclopedia—just a few lived-in details.

Prompt: *"What traditions might a village have around seasonal magic they depend on to survive?"*

These small rituals and customs breathe life into your setting.

Anchor Characters in Emotional Truth

Even if your hero is half-angel, raised by wolves, and carrying a sword forged from moonlight, we care about them because they're **emotionally honest**. They doubt. They fear. They long. That's what makes them real.

Use ChatGPT to explore: *"What internal conflict would a character have if they were trained to kill but want to heal?"*

or

"Describe how a chosen one might secretly resent their role."

Characters feel real when they're not perfect—when they want something, fear something, and struggle with what it means to be themselves.

Ask: *"Give me a quiet scene where the hero questions if they're doing the right thing."*

These moments might not involve action, but they carry *weight*. That's what sticks.

Let Relationships Evolve Naturally

One of the fastest ways to make fantasy feel artificial is to force relationships. Love at first swordfight. Hatred that turns to love with no middle ground. Trust that appears out of nowhere.

Slow it down—even in fast drafting.

Prompt: *"Write a scene where a knight and a rogue begin to trust each other after surviving something terrifying."*

You can also explore: *"What kind of tension would grow between a mage who hides their power and a friend who's been searching for a magical ally?"*

These aren't just interactions. They're emotional arcs. They're what make your world breathe.

Keep Stakes Human

Yes, kingdoms can rise and fall. But the stakes that hook readers are often smaller: one character's safety, one secret kept or revealed, one chance at freedom. When you zoom in emotionally, the world feels real—even if it's wrapped in magic.

Try this: *"Describe a moment where a character chooses to protect a friend over completing their quest, and it changes everything."*

Or: *"Show how losing a loved one affects the way a character casts magic from now on."*

These kinds of moments *live inside the reader*—and they make your story unforgettable.

Use Details with Purpose

You don't need pages of exposition to create realism. Just a few **specific, sensory details** do the job. A cracked teacup passed down for generations. The smell of sulfur that always follows a spell. The rough edge of a map that's been folded too many times.

Ask: *"Give me sensory details for a village that's survived five harsh winters and one dragon raid."*

Or: *"What small, repeated actions might a character do when preparing to cast a dangerous spell they learned in childhood?"*

Realism is in the repetition. The worn-in. The personal.

Let Conflict Come from Culture, Not Just Combat

Fantasy often leans on war and violence—but real tension can come from cultural pressure, family shame, moral dilemmas, or conflicting traditions.

Prompt ChatGPT: *"Write a conflict between a mage and a priest where both believe they're protecting the same village in different ways."*

You can also ask: *"What kind of ethical tension might arise in a kingdom where resurrection magic is only available to the rich?"*

These layers add complexity, realism, and emotional weight.

Let the Past Cast Shadows

Real worlds carry history. So should your fantasy. Not in lore dumps—but in scars. In ruins. In old songs and laws no one questions anymore.

Try: *"Write a scene where a character stumbles into a place touched by a forgotten war—and remembers something they were taught to forget."*

Or: *"Describe how the events of a magical rebellion 100 years ago still shape people's behavior today."*

Your story feels more real when the past isn't just backstory—it's **still shaping the present**.

When you want your fantasy to feel real, don't focus on making everything make sense. Focus on making everything feel *true*. Truth is what anchors the dragons, the runes, the ancient swords. Truth is what makes readers care.

Use ChatGPT to dig into the **emotional logic**, the **cultural texture**, and the **human cost** of every magical decision, every heroic act, every whispered prophecy. Ask questions. Try rewrites. Push for clarity and feeling. That's how a fantasy world becomes more than fiction—it becomes memory.

Adding the Unexpected: Surprise Events and Sudden Turns

Fantasy stories thrive on the unexpected. We read them to be transported to other worlds, but what keeps us turning the pages is surprise—moments that knock the wind out of us, shift the stakes, or reveal that things are not what they seemed. A good twist or surprise event doesn't just shock—it *changes the direction* of the story. It can force a character to grow, break an alliance, open a new mystery, or pull the rug out from under a reader's feet. And when you're writing fast, as you are in a one-day fantasy draft, using surprise well can give your story energy and freshness without slowing your pace.

Surprise, when done right, doesn't feel random. It feels like a detour you never saw coming, but realize in hindsight was inevitable. And the great news is, ChatGPT is an ideal partner for brainstorming the unexpected. With the right prompts, you can generate creative, genre-fitting surprises that feel organic and impactful, even if you're working on the fly.

What Counts as a Good Surprise?

In fantasy, surprises aren't just plot twists. They can be emotional reveals, magical anomalies, or sudden changes in loyalty. The key is that they must be:

- **Rooted** in what has come before
- **Disruptive** to the current momentum
- **Meaningful** to the character arcs or world logic

A good surprise should cause a character to reevaluate a choice, trigger a new chain of events, or uncover a deeper layer of conflict.

Try asking: *"Give me five surprising events that could happen during a fantasy quest without feeling random."*

or

"What's a magical event that could interrupt a wedding in a high-fantasy world?"

ChatGPT will return suggestions that can spark momentum mid-draft.

Surprise through Character

One of the most powerful ways to create surprise is through characters making *unexpected choices*. A sidekick betrays the hero. A feared enemy turns out to be a protector. A timid character reveals they've been manipulating events all along.

Prompt examples: *"What's a subtle way for a mentor character to be revealed as the real antagonist?"*

or

"How could a comic relief character suddenly become the story's moral center?"

These reversals make the world feel layered—and challenge your characters to adapt.

Surprise through Magic

Fantasy gives you a secret weapon: **unpredictable magic**. Even if your system is logical, it can still contain anomalies, ancient rules no one fully understands, or side effects that manifest under rare conditions.

Ask: *"What's a magical consequence of casting a spell too close to a sacred site?"*

"Describe an unexpected magical malfunction that occurs during a duel."

Sudden magical phenomena can create immediate danger—or open new narrative paths.

Surprises in magic can also come from broken rules. What happens when a forbidden spell is accidentally triggered? Or when a magical object is revealed to be alive?

Surprise through Setting

Your environment can flip the script too. The hidden city isn't empty—it's watching. The oasis is an illusion. The storm doesn't bring rain, it brings creatures.

Ask: *"What is an unexpected event that could occur when characters arrive at a long-lost ruin?"*

"Create a setting-based twist where geography is altered by a magical event."

Let the world behave strangely—but within the logic of your story.

Surprise through Revealed Truths

Sometimes, the biggest twists are information. A revelation about the past. A prophecy that was misinterpreted. A character's true heritage. These kinds of surprises often tie directly into the themes of identity, legacy, or destiny.

Ask: *"What's a twist about a royal bloodline that redefines the hero's place in the story?"*

"Give me a character secret that could change the reader's entire understanding of their behavior."

These kinds of twists make the world feel deep and lived-in.

Structuring the Surprise

Where should surprises land in your one-day draft?

- In the **first act**, a surprise might shift the protagonist's goal or understanding of their quest.
- In the **middle**, a betrayal or new magical complication keeps tension high.
- Near the **end**, a twist should reframe the final conflict or force a difficult decision.

You can even ask ChatGPT: *"What's a good midpoint twist for a fantasy story about a kingdom built on a lie?"*

or

"Suggest a final-act surprise that changes the meaning of the hero's journey."

These help you plan surprises into your outline—even late in the game.

Balancing Surprise with Satisfaction

The trick with surprises is not to outsmart your reader—it's to give them the gift of *realization*. The best twists land when the reader thinks, *Of course. I should have seen that.* They feel inevitable, not arbitrary.

So always ask:

- Does this twist come from character or world logic?
- Have I hinted at it, even if subtly?
- Does it challenge what the characters believe about themselves or their world?

If yes, it's more than a twist—it's a **turning point**.

In a one-day draft, surprises are fuel. They can reignite a scene that's starting to sag. They can solve a pacing problem or set up a new arc. And with ChatGPT, you can throw in creative turns without pausing the flow.

Ask often. Experiment freely. Twist wisely.

Because in fantasy, the unexpected isn't just part of the journey—it's what makes the journey unforgettable.

Formatting and Saving Your Story for Publishing

You did it. You've written your fantasy story in a single day—from the first spark of a magical idea to the final echo of your story's last line. Now, it's time to take that raw creative energy and **prepare it for the world**. Whether you're planning to self-publish, share it on a blog, submit it to a magazine, or just send it to a friend, **formatting and saving your story properly** makes a huge difference in how it's received. Presentation isn't just polish—it's respect for your work and for your reader.

In this chapter, we'll walk through the steps to clean up, format, and save your fantasy manuscript for publishing or sharing. You don't need to be a tech wizard. With ChatGPT at your side, it's faster and simpler than you think.

Step One: Decide Your Destination

Before you format, figure out *where* your story is going. Different platforms have different formatting needs.

Are you:

- Self-Publishing to Kindle Direct Publishing (KDP), Draft2Digital or other Sites?
- Creating a downloadable PDF for your website or mailing list?
- Formatting for print (paperback or hardcover)?
- Sharing on a site like Wattpad or Substack?
- Sending to beta readers or editors?

Once you know the destination, you can tailor the file and layout accordingly.

Ask ChatGPT: *"What are the standard formatting requirements for submitting a short fantasy novel to Amazon KDP?"*

or

"Help me format a fantasy story for Substack with clean headings and scene breaks."

You'll get guidance that fits your goal.

Step Two: Choose the Right File Format

Here's a quick guide:

- **.DOCX or .DOC** – Great for editing, collaborating, or submitting to agents/publishers.
- **.PDF** – Best for fixed formatting, sharing with beta readers, or creating digital ARCs.
- **.EPUB or .MOBI** – Required for eBook distribution platforms like KDP or Smashwords.
- **.TXT or Markdown (.md)** – Useful for blogs or clean HTML conversion.
- **.HTML** – Needed if you're uploading directly to websites with styling.

Ask: *"How do I convert my Word document into a clean EPUB file for publishing?"*

ChatGPT can walk you through using tools like Calibre, Reedsy, or Vellum.

Step Three: Standard Manuscript Formatting

If you're sending your story to publishers, contests, or readers who expect traditional formatting, follow this classic structure:

- 12-point **Times New Roman** or **Garamond**
- Double-spaced lines
- 1-inch margins on all sides
- Left-aligned text (no justified alignment)
- Header with your name / title / page number
- Start new chapters on a new page

Prompt example: *"Format this story in standard manuscript layout with proper scene breaks and chapter headings."*

ChatGPT can auto-format sample sections or help generate style sheets.

Step Four: Use Clean Scene and Chapter Breaks

In fantasy, scene breaks are common—time skips, magical transitions, or point-of-view shifts. Use a consistent symbol to show these breaks:

- Three centered asterisks (***)
- A decorative symbol (❧ or §)
- Extra space between paragraphs

Prompt: *"Replace all scene transitions in my story with centered asterisks and space them properly."*

Or: *"Format each chapter with a clear heading: 'Chapter One: The Forest of Echoes.'"*

Clean structure keeps your reader anchored—even when the world is wild.

Step Five: Create a Title Page and Table of Contents

For eBooks or longer works, you'll want:

- A title page (with title, subtitle, author name)
- Optional copyright or disclaimer
- A clickable Table of Contents (for EPUBs and PDFs)

Ask: *"Generate a fantasy-style title page for a story called The Fire That Remembers."*

or

"Create a clickable Table of Contents with 10 chapters and epilogue."

This makes your story feel like a *book*, not just a document.

Step Six: Save Versions Strategically

Save your story in multiple formats:

- The editable original (.docx or .pages)
- A polished shareable PDF
- An eBook version (EPUB or MOBI if needed)
- A plain-text backup (.txt or .md)

Also, **name your files clearly**, with version numbers:

- *WhispersOfTheDeep_V1.docx*
- *WhispersOfTheDeep_FINAL.pdf*
- *WhispersOfTheDeep_KDP.epub*

Prompt ChatGPT: *"Help me create a folder structure to organize my fantasy writing drafts, versions, and publishing assets."*

Being organized now saves time (and sanity) later.

Step Seven: Run a Quick Formatting Proof

Before you hit upload or share:

- Do a scroll-through to check for strange breaks, font issues, or spacing gaps.
- Skim for repeated words or leftover placeholder names.
- Check the final chapter for a satisfying finish and a clean exit.

Ask: *"Can you review this formatted draft and identify any layout or formatting inconsistencies?"*

Even just having AI walk through your structure line-by-line helps catch the small stuff.

In the end, formatting is about **respecting the story you've just written**. You raced through worlds and wrote with fire. Now give your story the structure it deserves so it can reach others clearly, cleanly, and beautifully.

You don't need a graphic designer or layout pro. You just need care, curiosity, and a few good prompts.

Cover Design and Blurb Writing with AI's Help

You've written your fantasy story in a day. You've formatted it, saved it, and it reads like a finished book. Now it's time to give it the final magic touch: **a cover and a blurb**. These two elements are your book's first impression. The cover catches the eye. The blurb seals the deal. They work together to convince a reader that your story is not only worth their attention—but that it might just become their new favorite escape.

The great news? You don't need a design degree or copywriting skills to get it done. With the help of ChatGPT, you can **create an eye-catching cover concept** and **craft a compelling blurb** that captures your story's tone, stakes, and heart. Let's break it down.

Step One: Blurb First, Cover Second

Even though the cover is visual, it helps to start with the **blurb**. Why? Because writing the blurb forces you to define what your story *is*—its genre, tone, theme, hook, and emotional pull. Once that's clear, you'll have a stronger vision for what the cover should represent.

Crafting a Blurb with ChatGPT

Your blurb has one job: **get the reader to open the book**. It should create curiosity, highlight the main character, introduce the central conflict, and promise some kind of journey or transformation.

Prompt example: *"Write a 150-word fantasy back cover blurb for a story about a healer who discovers she's the last living bloodline of a tyrant king."*

You'll often get something like:

In the shattered kingdom of Vaelor, seventeen-year-old Maeve has lived her life in the shadows—healing the sick, hiding her name, and avoiding the ruins of her family's legacy. But when an injured soldier arrives bearing a ring etched with the royal crest, her past comes roaring back.

Maeve is the last of the Bloodmarked. And someone wants her dead before she remembers why.

As ancient magic stirs and forgotten allies rise, Maeve must choose: bury the bloodline that destroyed a kingdom—or rise with it and claim what was once hers.

Then you can refine it by asking: *"Make the tone more dark and lyrical."*

"Add more tension and mystery without revealing too much."

"Rewrite it in a first-person voice."

You can create multiple versions and test which one fits the *feeling* of your story best.

Blurb Structure Tips

If you're writing or revising the blurb manually, here's a common format:

1. **Introduce the protagonist and their normal world**
2. **Hint at the disruption or problem**
3. **Introduce stakes and decisions**
4. **Close with a hook or promise of what's to come**

Let ChatGPT help at each step with: *"Summarize my story's core conflict in one sentence."*

"What's a strong final line for a fantasy back cover blurb?"

These pieces help you create a blurb that works like a well-cast spell: short, potent, and impossible to ignore.

Designing a Cover with AI's Guidance

Now that you know your story's tone and hook, you can focus on **visual storytelling**. Your fantasy cover doesn't need to look like a blockbuster movie poster. It just needs to:

- Reflect your genre and tone (epic, dark, romantic, whimsical, grim)
- Evoke curiosity
- Be visually clean and readable, especially at thumbnail size

Start by asking: *"Describe a fantasy book cover idea for a story about a city built in the ribcage of a dead god."*

or

"What are some iconic fantasy imagery elements that match a romantic fantasy with a dark twist?"

You might get ideas like:

- A sword wrapped in vines, with blood dripping from the hilt
- A single eye glowing from beneath a shattered crown
- A heroine standing on ruins with magical light swirling around her

Use these ideas to either design your own cover (via Canva or Photoshop) or describe your vision to an AI image generator or designer.

Use ChatGPT for Title Design Tips

Even your title can benefit from a bit of AI inspiration. Ask: *"Suggest five fantasy titles based on this blurb."*

or

"Which title fits best for a tragic, character-driven fantasy about lost heritage?"

Titles are a part of your cover, and they need to fit the tone just as much as the imagery.

Tools to Create the Final Cover

If you're doing the design yourself, here are tools you can use:

- **Canva** (free templates, drag-and-drop tools, fantasy-style fonts)
- **BookBrush** (designed specifically for authors)
- **AI Image Generators** (like DALL·E, MidJourney, or Bing Image Creator for concept art)
- **Photoshop** (for more advanced users)

You can also ask ChatGPT: *"What size should I make my book cover for Amazon KDP?"*

or

"Give me a fantasy color palette for a dark romantic adventure story."

The key is simplicity and legibility. Your title should pop, the image should tell a story, and the vibe should match the genre your reader expects.

Final Touch: The Tagline

Want a quick hook right under the title? Add a tagline.

Ask ChatGPT: *"Give me five fantasy taglines for a story about a warrior who must betray her kingdom to save it."*

You'll get short, sharp lines like:

- *Loyalty can be treason in disguise.*
- *The crown is hers. The blood is theirs.*
- *Every empire begins with a broken oath.*

Taglines are optional—but powerful.

Your blurb and cover are your book's **invitation**. They're the spell that opens the door to your world. With ChatGPT, you don't have to face the blank page or blank canvas alone. You can brainstorm fast, refine creatively, and walk away with a back cover and visual that do justice to the fantasy you wrote in just one day.

Sharing, Selling, or Just Savouring Your Finished Fantasy

You've done what many only dream of: you created a fantasy story from start to finish—in a single day. You imagined new worlds, conjured magic systems, built characters who bleed and burn and grow, and now you're staring at something real. A story that exists. A draft with weight. So what's next?

Some writers sprint to publish. Others tuck their work away like a secret relic. Some share it with a trusted few. Others build an empire from a one-day tale. There's no right answer. What matters is that your story now *has a life*. In this chapter, we'll explore the options: how to share your finished story, how to sell it if you choose, and how to simply savor the magic of completion—because not every story needs to be sold to be meaningful.

Share It with a Circle That Cares

Sometimes, the most powerful moment after writing a story is letting someone else read it. A friend. A fellow writer. A fantasy fan you trust. You don't need a website, a marketing plan, or a publisher to hit "send."

Ask ChatGPT to help you: *"Write a short email introducing my one-day fantasy story to beta readers."*

or

"Create a fun social media post to share my fantasy draft with friends."

You can attach a PDF, paste it into Google Docs, or read it aloud. The point is not polish—it's *presence*. You made something. That's worth sharing.

Publish It Digitally (Even Rough)

Platforms like **Draft2Digital, Wattpad**, **Substack**, **Medium**, or your own blog are great places to post fantasy stories, even first drafts. Many readers love rough stories—they feel raw, immediate, alive. You can even publish in parts, releasing a chapter a day or week.

Prompt ChatGPT: *"Help me write an intro paragraph for my fantasy story post on Substack."*

or

"Give me a summary and genre tags for posting this story to Wattpad."

Then format your story (Chapter 57) and publish with confidence. You might be surprised by how many people love early drafts—because they invite others into the creative journey.

Self-Publish as an eBook or Print Book

Ready to take a bigger step? You can turn your one-day draft into a Kindle ebook or even a paperback through Amazon's **KDP**, Smashwords, or Draft2Digital.

ChatGPT can help: *"Write my Amazon book description based on this blurb."*

"What categories should I list my fantasy story under on KDP?"

You can design a quick cover (Chapter 58), format your manuscript, and publish in under an hour. Yes, *that* fast.

You can also turn it into a free downloadable ebook to use for growing a mailing list or offering as a reader magnet.

Ask: *"How do I convert my Word doc into an EPUB for free?"*

or

"Give me steps to upload my fantasy book to Amazon KDP."

This isn't about perfection—it's about presence. And presence builds momentum.

Build a Series from What You Wrote

One of the best surprises in finishing a one-day story is realizing it could be *more*. Maybe that side character deserves a spinoff. Maybe the villain's origin needs exploring. Maybe this story was just the first legend in a whole world of sagas.

Ask ChatGPT: *"Based on this fantasy story, what are five possible sequel ideas?"*

or

"How could I turn this into a fantasy serial for email subscribers?"

Suddenly, today's story becomes the seed of tomorrow's series. One day of writing becomes a chapter in something far bigger.

Savour It. Reflect. Celebrate.

You don't *have* to share or sell it. You can just read it back. Let yourself feel what you built. Highlight lines you love. Notice the themes you didn't plan but somehow found. Revisit your favorite moment. This is what it means to be a writer: you made something from nothing. You wrote into a void—and now there's a story where there wasn't one before.

Ask ChatGPT: *"Help me write a short reflection on finishing my one-day fantasy story."*

This kind of journaling can be powerful. It helps you remember how it felt. Why it mattered. And why you'll do it again.

You can also keep a "finished stories" folder and drop your draft in it like placing a gem on a shelf.

Sometimes, savouring is the most satisfying ending of all.

Whether you decide to share your story with the world, polish it into something to sell, or keep it close to your chest like a treasured spell-book, you've already done something remarkable. You created. You completed. You didn't wait. You wrote the fantasy story that was in you.

And the best part? Now you know you can do it again.

Examples of Good Prompts for Fantasy Story Design and Structure

Prompts are where magic begins. A blank page can feel overwhelming, but the right question—aimed at the right angle—can unlock an entire world. Whether you're building a sweeping epic, a one-day adventure, or a dark little tale that slips in under the skin, your prompts guide the process. With ChatGPT, the key to writing strong fantasy isn't just asking *what happens next*—it's learning how to ask smarter, deeper, more specific questions that lead to emotionally rich and logically sound storytelling.

In this final chapter, we're going to load you up with **powerful fantasy story prompts**—designed for idea generation, structure building, twist creation, world development, and character arcs. Use them in your next project, modify them for fun, or even paste them directly into ChatGPT when you're stuck. Each one is a springboard.

Idea Generation and Core Concept Prompts

Start here when you're looking for the bones of your story:

- *"Give me five fantasy story ideas where the magic system is based on memory, and forgetting is the price of power."*
- *"What would a fantasy story look like if the protagonist was a villain in a previous life trying to undo their legacy?"*
- *"Create a fantasy plot centered on a kingdom that must rely on an ancient enemy for survival."*
- *"Suggest story ideas where nature itself becomes sentient and wages war on civilization."*
- *"What kind of story could take place in a world where time only flows forward for some people and backward for others?"*

These prompts help you build a foundation that's unusual but full of depth and potential conflict.

Story Structure and Three-Act Design Prompts

When you've got an idea but need to shape it:

- *"Outline a three-act fantasy story structure for a reluctant hero who discovers they are the final piece in a prophecy."*
- *"Break down a five-beat plot structure for a fantasy novella where a thief accidentally steals a cursed relic."*
- *"Structure a fantasy story using the Hero's Journey but make the 'Refusal of the Call' moment last an entire act."*
- *"How would a fantasy story unfold if it started with the ending and worked backward through time?"*
- *"Outline the story beats for a fantasy political thriller set in a city where magic is banned."*

These help keep your pacing sharp, your progression logical, and your stakes escalating.

Worldbuilding and Setting Prompts

Use these to breathe life into your fantasy universe:

- *"Describe a fantasy city built inside the skeleton of a fallen god—what's its culture, economy, and magic like?"*
- *"Invent a desert-based fantasy culture with unique traditions, politics, and magical beliefs."*
- *"What kind of religion would evolve in a world where stars are living beings that can fall to the earth?"*
- *"Describe three regions of a fantasy continent—each with its own elemental alignment, history, and natural*

dangers."

- *"What are five local legends that exist in a small village on the edge of a cursed forest?"*

These make your world feel real, immersive, and unforgettable.

Magic System and Lore Prompts

Create consistency, originality, and consequences:

- *"Design a magic system where spells require a blood tie between caster and subject—what rules and loopholes arise?"*
- *"What would a magic school look like in a world where all magic is based on emotional trauma?"*
- *"Create a mythology around the moon phases and how they affect divine intervention in mortal affairs."*
- *"Describe forbidden branches of magic in a kingdom where necromancy is considered divine."*
- *"What magical side effects could result from improperly cast spells that bind the soul?"*

These deepen your story's logic and give you tools to build conflict organically.

Character Arcs and Relationship Prompts

For dynamic heroes, villains, and emotional growth:

- *"What internal struggle might a hero face if their greatest power only activates when they feel guilt?"*
- *"Create a character arc for a mentor who is slowly losing faith in magic while training a prodigy."*
- *"What would cause a lifelong friendship between a knight and a mage to fracture right before the final battle?"*
- *"How might a villain change if they were forced to raise the hero's child?"*
- *"Describe a love story between two characters on opposite sides of a war who are each hiding a magical secret."*

Emotionally driven prompts like these make your fantasy feel grounded and powerful.

Plot Twist and Conflict-Building Prompts

Perfect when your story needs more tension or surprise:

- *"What's a fantasy plot twist that could make the protagonist question whether they're the real villain?"*
- *"Describe a sudden betrayal that would split a fantasy adventuring party in half."*
- *"What kind of secret could a kingdom be hiding that, once revealed, would change everything about the hero's mission?"*
- *"Give me an unexpected magical consequence that turns a victory into a disaster."*
- *"Design a subplot where a character's magic starts hurting them, but they're too afraid to stop using it."*

Twists give your story texture. Prompts like these turn predictable tales into page-turners.

Final Inspirational Prompt Sets

To kickstart your next fantasy story from scratch:

- *"Give me ten fantasy story concepts that each revolve around a single powerful object—one sacred, one cursed, one misunderstood."*
- *"List five opening scenes for fantasy novels that hook the reader immediately."*
- *"Describe a fantasy world where death doesn't exist—only transformation. What kind of story could take place there?"*
- *"Suggest fantasy story structures that break from the traditional quest format."*
- *"Create a fantasy story pitch that blends dark academia, elemental magic, and political rebellion."*

Use them as-is, or remix them to match your style.

Prompts aren't a sign you're out of ideas. They're the flint and steel that light the fire. They help you think sideways, dig deeper, and explore possibilities that weren't obvious before. With the right prompt, a single sentence can become a trilogy. A tiny spark can explode into a whole world.

Now that you've completed your one-day fantasy writing journey—and have the tools to write faster, smarter, and with more soul—you can come back to this chapter anytime you need to begin again.

And you will. Because one story always leads to the next.

So take a breath. Choose a prompt. Open a new page.

The next world is waiting.

Examples of Good Prompts for Designing Compelling Characters

A great fantasy story doesn't just need magic, monsters, and ancient prophecies—it needs *people.* Characters are the soul of your world. They're the ones who carry the weight of fate, clash with destiny, break curses, and make impossible choices. But the most unforgettable characters aren't just cool or powerful—they're **complicated**. They have beliefs, fears, longings, and flaws. They *change.* And when you're writing a story in one day, crafting compelling characters quickly is about asking the **right questions**.

That's where prompts come in.

ChatGPT can help you build deep, vivid, emotionally resonant characters in minutes if you guide it with smart, targeted prompts. Below are examples you can use at every stage of character development—hero, villain, mentor, rogue, royalty, rebel—whether you're starting from scratch or deepening an existing arc.

Prompts for Creating Protagonists

Start with who they are, what they want, and why they can't have it.

- *"Create a fantasy protagonist who is terrified of their own magical abilities—but must use them to save someone they love."*
- *"Design a reluctant hero from a noble bloodline who wants nothing more than a quiet life, but is forced into politics by a hidden betrayal."*
- *"Give me a character who is trained to be a killer but has never taken a life—yet everyone around them assumes they have."*
- *"Build a protagonist whose moral code puts them at odds with the people they must protect."*
- *"What is a fantasy character archetype I can turn upside down to create something fresh but familiar?"*

These get to the core: motivation, conflict, and internal contradiction.

Prompts for Building Villains with Depth

Villains become unforgettable when they believe they're the hero of the story.

- *"Create a fantasy villain who is trying to prevent a prophecy from coming true—but doesn't realize they're causing it."*
- *"Design an antagonist who is driven by love for someone who's already gone, and will destroy anything to bring them back."*
- *"Write a sympathetic villain whose greatest flaw is their refusal to forgive themselves."*
- *"Describe a tyrant who rose to power by solving a real crisis—and fears losing control more than death."*
- *"What does a morally gray antagonist look like in a world where good and evil are determined by magical alignment?"*

Let ChatGPT help you create villains readers *understand*, even if they don't agree.

Prompts for Side Characters Who Steal the Show

Secondary characters often carry the heart—or the heartbreak—of your story.

- *"Give me a fantasy sidekick who secretly wants to be the hero but is too afraid to lead."*
- *"Describe a mentor who knows they're dying and is hiding it from their student."*
- *"Build a comic relief character who hides their sorrow behind every joke."*
- *"What kind of backstory would a stoic warrior have if they refuse to ever unsheathe their sword again?"*
- *"Create a rogue character whose charm masks a deep, unresolved betrayal."*

These kinds of characters add flavor, tension, and emotion to every scene.

Prompts for Designing Group Dynamics

Fantasy thrives on found families, rivalries, and uneasy alliances.

- *"What kind of group conflict might erupt between a priest, a necromancer, and a royal guard on a shared quest?"*
- *"Design a fantasy adventuring party where each member has a reason to betray the others—but hasn't yet."*
- *"Describe how a character changes when they're forced to lead a group they don't respect."*
- *"Give me emotional tension between two siblings who must protect each other but don't speak anymore."*
- *"Create a trio of fantasy characters where each one is hiding something from the others."*

These prompts help you write not just individuals, but **relationships** that evolve under pressure.

Prompts for Internal Conflict and Growth

Character arcs are what turn fantasy into **myth**. Use prompts to challenge and reshape your heroes.

- *"What lie does this character believe about themselves, and what moment proves it wrong?"*
- *"How does a character who swore never to use magic again end up using it to save their enemy?"*
- *"Describe a moment where a character must choose between the person they love and the cause they've sworn to."*
- *"Create a character arc where someone goes from obedient follower to revolutionary leader."*
- *"What happens when a healer's magic begins to hurt those they try to save?"*

These questions dig beneath the surface and fuel emotional turning points.

Prompts for Physical, Cultural, and Magical Uniqueness

Details make characters memorable—and world-specific.

- *"Design a fantasy character whose appearance is marked by the side effects of their magic."*
- *"Create a character from a culture that believes names hold power—so they use a false name in public."*
- *"Give me five physical or behavioral traits for a warrior raised underwater."*
- *"Describe how a character's magical bond to an animal affects their mood and choices."*
- *"What are the unique gestures, clothing, or beliefs of a person raised in a city where dreams are currency?"*

Prompts like these help ensure your characters *belong* in the world you've built.

Remember, you don't have to know your character's whole backstory before you start writing. You just need an angle. A spark. An edge to hold onto. The right prompt can turn a vague idea into a character who walks off the page.

Ask often. Revise freely. Let ChatGPT help you challenge what you think you know about your characters. Because when they surprise you, they'll surprise your readers too.

In the next chapter, we'll explore **examples of good prompts for world building**—so your characters have a vivid, living realm to journey through, rise in, and maybe even save.

Examples of Good Prompts for World Building

World building is the soul of fantasy. It's the architecture behind your story—the language in a rebel's prayer, the color of the sky at twilight, the reason a village places stones outside its door during the full moon. When done well, a fantasy world feels not just imagined, but *lived in*. And whether you're writing a sweeping epic or a one-day short story, world building doesn't have to take months. With the right prompts, especially when using ChatGPT, you can create immersive, layered worlds in minutes.

In this chapter, you'll find a treasure chest of world-building prompts organized by category: geography, society, magic, history, culture, economy, politics, religion, and daily life. Use them to shape your world quickly—or dive deeper into your existing one. The only limit is how far you're willing to imagine.

Geography and Setting Prompts

These prompts help shape the physical structure of your world:

- *"Describe a continent where one side floats in the sky and the other is buried under the sea. How do its people survive?"*
- *"Give me five unique terrains for a fantasy world that has no sun, only starlight."*
- *"Create a mountain range where each peak is home to a different species or magical order."*
- *"What kind of world would evolve in a place where gravity is unstable?"*
- *"Design a border town between a realm of fire and a forest that dreams."*

These spark settings that inspire mood, culture, and conflict.

Magic and Power Systems Prompts

Craft logic and wonder in equal measure:

- *"Design a magic system based on the four classical elements, but each element is tied to a personality trait."*
- *"What are the consequences of casting magic that drains memories?"*
- *"Create a forbidden school of magic that was outlawed after a magical war—but still secretly taught."*
- *"In a world where magic is powered by grief, how do societies treat mourning?"*
- *"What are five magical limitations that make powerful spells risky to use?"*

Great magic systems aren't just powerful—they're **personal** and **dangerous**.

Cultural and Social Structure Prompts

This is where the world becomes *alive* through behavior and belief:

- *"What holidays or rituals might exist in a floating city that fears falling?"*
- *"Describe a marriage tradition in a desert culture where water is sacred."*
- *"What social rules might exist in a society where everyone is born with a prophecy?"*
- *"How do different cultures in your world treat death—and what magic surrounds burial?"*
- *"Create a naming system based on a person's greatest failure or accomplishment."*

Cultural prompts allow small moments to echo through generations.

Politics, Kingdoms, and Factions Prompts

These help you build tension and structure:

- *"What political system would exist in a city where the ruling family cannot speak?"*
- *"Describe three rival factions in a magical academy and what each believes about power."*
- *"Create a council made up of representatives from extinct races, each one magically resurrected for one day a year."*
- *"What are the effects of a magical caste system where power is inherited through blood?"*
- *"Give me the laws of a kingdom that worships chaos."*

Fantasy politics gives your world conflict, secrets, and high stakes.

Religion, Myth, and Belief System Prompts

Worldviews shape everything:

- *"Invent a religion based on stars that fall to earth as omens."*
- *"What myths would form in a world where the gods live among mortals, but only speak to children?"*
- *"Design a belief system where forgetting is considered holy."*
- *"What kind of cult would worship decay as a form of rebirth?"*
- *"Create a pantheon of gods, each one bound to a different time of day."*

Belief systems make even the mundane feel magical.

History, Lore, and Legends Prompts

The past deepens the present:

- *"Write a legend about the first dragon, and why it vanished."*
- *"What event led to the collapse of the world's greatest magical city—and what do people say still lives in its ruins?"*
- *"Describe an ancient war that split the world into two opposing magical philosophies."*
- *"What artifact changed the course of history, and who controls it now?"*
- *"How has a long-dead hero's legacy been distorted across the centuries?"*

When your world has a memory, your story gains gravity.

Economy, Trade, and Daily Life Prompts

Ground your fantasy world with relatable—and strange—details:

- *"What form of currency would exist in a world where time is a measurable substance?"*
- *"Describe what a fantasy street market smells like on a rainy day."*
- *"What is the most prized non-magical item in your world, and why?"*
- *"Create a system of trade between a subterranean kingdom and a sky-dwelling empire."*
- *"How do ordinary people make a living in a city built on ancient magical ruins?"*

Daily life is the heartbeat of your world—it makes the magic believable.

Conflict and Tension Prompts

Drama shapes the world as much as geography:

- *"What cultural tension exists between two neighboring kingdoms who share a god but interpret it differently?"*
- *"How does a suppressed magical minority resist in a kingdom that hunts them?"*
- *"What secret war is being fought beneath the surface of daily life—and who knows the truth?"*
- *"Design a border conflict that arises from a magical storm shifting the land overnight."*
- *"Who benefits from a magical illness—and who's trying to cure it?"*

Tension = plot fuel. These ideas make the world *move*.

Bonus: Starting-From-Nothing Prompts

Need a random world generator? Try:

- *"Give me a completely original fantasy world idea including geography, dominant species, power source, major conflict, and a legend that still shapes daily life."*
- *"Create a fantasy setting for a tragic romance between a ghost and a monster-hunter."*
- *"Design a fantasy world inspired by ocean trench ecosystems, lost empires, and memory-based magic."*
- *"What would a fantasy world look like if the moon were alive and jealous of the sun?"*
- *"Describe a world where war is fought not with armies, but with dreams."*

These can start an entire story—or an entire series.

World building is never about dumping facts—it's about creating a place worth exploring. A few strong details can do more than a thousand-page map. And with ChatGPT, you can build fast and deep, layering logic, history, and wonder into every scene.

Let your questions lead the way. Keep digging. Keep dreaming. Because somewhere in the fog of prompts and possibilities, there's a world only *you* can bring to life.

In the next chapter, we'll explore **examples of good prompts for ideas about fantasy stories**—the sparks that ignite the next tale, whether you're starting fresh or building out a whole series.

Examples of Good Prompts for Ideas about Fantasy Stories

Every fantasy story begins with a question, a "what if," or a strange little seed that refuses to go away. But sometimes, staring at the blank page, it's hard to conjure anything but fog. That's where prompts come in—not to give you *the* story, but to help you discover *your* story. The right prompt can open a portal. With ChatGPT as your creative partner, you can spark dozens of fantasy ideas in a single session, each one ready to become your next epic, novella, or one-day writing challenge.

This chapter is a well of powerful, flexible prompts. Use them to start fresh, to break a writing block, or to build out a fantasy series. Some are concept-driven. Some are character-first. Some are pure mood. But all of them are designed to help you generate **fantasy stories that feel alive**—with magic, mystery, emotion, and meaning.

Core Concept Prompts

These help you come up with unique world setups and story hooks.

- *"Give me a fantasy story idea where people can see the moment they die—but not how."*
- *"What happens in a world where every child is born with a magical scar that reveals their fate?"*
- *"Create a fantasy story set in a realm where music is used to control memory."*
- *"What would a society look like if dreams determined your social status?"*
- *"Design a story where a magical storm returns every 100 years—and the main character is the only one who remembers the last one."*

These build big-picture wonder and thematic richness right from the start.

Character-Driven Prompts

Start with someone unforgettable, then build the world around them.

- *"Create a fantasy story about a warrior who has never lost a battle—but was cursed to forget every victory."*
- *"Tell the story of a healer who can only cure others by taking on their wounds."*
- *"Write a fantasy story where a thief steals a crown and accidentally becomes king of a forgotten kingdom."*
- *"What happens when a necromancer falls in love with one of the spirits they summoned?"*
- *"Describe a reluctant chosen one who fakes their own death to escape destiny."*

Compelling characters drive everything—they're the beating heart of every world.

Conflict and Dilemma Prompts

Fantasy thrives on impossible choices and dangerous power.

- *"What happens when two rival kingdoms learn they share the same ancestral god—and the god awakens?"*
- *"Write a fantasy story about a rebellion inside a magic school where the students outpower the masters."*
- *"Create a story where an enchanted weapon chooses a new wielder every year—and each one dies trying to use it."*
- *"Describe a peace treaty that hinges on a marriage between enemies—but one is cursed."*
- *"Tell the story of a prophecy meant to save the world—but the only way to fulfill it is through total destruction."*

Great conflict drives plot and reveals character under pressure.

Setting-Based Prompts

Start with the world, then see who lives in it—and what they want.

- *"Write a fantasy story set in a floating monastery above a land torn by war."*
- *"Create a city built inside the skeleton of a god—and explore what secrets still stir in the bones."*
- *"Describe life in a kingdom where seasons are controlled by competing elemental spirits."*
- *"Tell a story set on an island that only appears during a blood moon."*
- *"Build a story around a forest where time runs backward."*

Settings can shape mood, pace, and theme—don't just decorate, **build story into place**.

Theme and Emotion Prompts

Start with feeling. These prompts anchor your story in the emotional truth behind the fantasy.

- *"Write a fantasy story about grief—where a character brings someone back, only to lose them again."*
- *"Create a hopeful story in a dying world, where one small act of magic starts a slow rebirth."*
- *"What does redemption look like in a world where your sins take physical form?"*
- *"Tell a story of forbidden love between a mortal and an elemental being who must forget each other to survive."*
- *"Explore the journey of a character who has everything—except freedom."*

Theme-forward stories tend to stick with readers long after the last page.

Genre-Twisting Prompts

Fantasy can blend with mystery, romance, horror, comedy, or sci-fi. Try cross-genre sparks:

- *"Write a fantasy mystery about a murdered dragon whose hoard contains a cursed map."*
- *"Tell a romantic fantasy where two characters can only meet once every hundred years—but fall in love in a single day."*
- *"Create a fantasy horror story about a village that worships a sleeping sea god—and the god wakes up."*
- *"What happens in a bureaucratic empire where spells must be notarized before they're cast?"*
- *"Build a magical courtroom drama about a witch accused of time theft."*

These add flavor and uniqueness to familiar fantasy frameworks.

Legend and Lore Prompts

Great fantasy stories often revolve around lost history, ancient prophecies, or forgotten truths.

- *"Write a fantasy tale where a myth turns out to be real—but twisted in the telling."*
- *"Create a story about a character who must relive the events of a famous legend to uncover what really happened."*
- *"Tell the story of a wandering storyteller who discovers the tale they're telling is about themselves."*
- *"What happens when an ancient artifact is discovered—and its true purpose was hidden for a reason?"*
- *"Explore a world where history is rewritten by magic—literally, books change."*

This adds weight and depth to your fantasy, turning stories into *myths*.

Random Generator Prompts

Let ChatGPT fully surprise you. Try:

- *"Give me five original fantasy story ideas based on a single object, one character, and one rule of magic."*
- *"Create a fantasy story based on the word 'ashes,' the emotion 'longing,' and the setting 'abandoned temple.'"*
- *"Suggest a fantasy plot inspired by Celtic mythology, space opera themes, and forbidden love."*
- *"Write a fantasy premise with a hero, an anti-hero, and a creature that doesn't believe in magic."*
- *"Generate a fantasy story idea where everything turns upside down halfway through."*

Random prompts = surprising stories.

The fantasy genre has no limits—only launching points. These prompts don't give you the whole map. They give you the compass, the fog, and just enough light to step forward. Let ChatGPT help you expand, twist, and reimagine what comes next. Because in fantasy, the most powerful magic is often the idea that refuses to leave you alone.

In the next chapter, we'll explore how to **turn a single prompt into a full one-day story plan**—with structure, character, setting, and a clear beginning, middle, and end.

Your One-Day Fantasy Writing Game Plan – From Start to Publish

Writing a fantasy story in a single day might sound like a mad dash through dragon-fire—but it's not only possible, it's wildly fun and creatively empowering. With the right rhythm, smart use of ChatGPT, and a clear focus, you can take a blank page and transform it into a finished, formatted, ready-to-publish fantasy story *in just one day*. This final chapter gives you your complete, step-by-step game plan—from spark to spellbinding story.

This isn't just a process—it's a **repeatable method**. Use it whenever you want to break through blocks, draft fast, or just prove to yourself that you're a one-day fantasy-writing machine.

Hour 1: The Idea Spark (8:00 AM – 9:00 AM)

Start with discovery. Use ChatGPT to generate ideas, answer key questions, and help you form the seed of your story.

Prompts to use:

- *"Give me five fantasy story concepts with a strong magical hook."*
- *"Build a quick summary about a cursed kingdom and a reluctant hero."*
- *"Create a character arc for a mage who's afraid of their own power."*

Before the hour ends, lock in:

- A protagonist with a problem
- A central conflict or twist
- A magical setting or system

You don't need a full outline. You just need direction.

Hour 2: Quick Structure + Beats (9:00 AM – 10:00 AM)

Map your story in simple beats.

Ask ChatGPT:

- *"Give me a three-act structure for this idea."*
- *"What's a good midpoint twist that changes everything?"*
- *"Help me write a one-line summary of each chapter for a 10-chapter novella."*

By the end of this hour, you'll have a roadmap. It doesn't have to be fancy—it just has to keep you moving.

Hours 3–6: Writing Act I (10:00 AM – 1:00 PM)

Start writing your opening. Let ChatGPT help with:

- Scene starters
- Descriptions
- Dialogue
- Emotional beats

Prompt ideas:

- *"Write the opening paragraph for a dark fantasy with lyrical tone."*
- *"Create a scene where the hero is forced to make a moral choice early on."*
- *"How can I make this dialogue feel more natural?"*

Write fast. Don't edit. Let it be messy. Just keep going.

Hour 7: Lunch + Recharge (1:00 PM – 2:00 PM)

Step away. Let the story simmer. Take a walk, eat something real, and let your mind drift. You've already built the bones of a new world.

Hours 8–10: Writing Act II (2:00 PM – 5:00 PM)

Return to the draft. Raise the stakes. Introduce betrayal, magic gone wrong, or internal struggle. Use ChatGPT to help craft:

- Midpoint reveals
- New characters
- Action sequences
- Emotional tension

Prompt examples:

- *"Write a scene where the villain turns out to be the hero's sibling."*
- *"Create a magical duel that escalates but ends with a twist."*

You'll likely pass the halfway point of your word count here. Keep up the pace.

Hours 11–12: Writing Act III (5:00 PM – 7:00 PM)

Now the endgame. Bring it all together.

Use ChatGPT for:

- Final battles or sacrifices
- Emotional resolution
- The closing image or last line

Prompt examples:

- *"Write a poetic ending where the hero chooses exile over glory."*
- *"Describe the climax where magic breaks the laws of the world."*

Don't worry if it's rough. Get to the end.

Hours 13–14: Editing Pass + Scene Fixes (7:00 PM – 9:00 PM)

Run a light pass over your draft. Focus on:

- Fixing awkward phrasing
- Checking for plot holes
- Strengthening character arcs
- Clarifying confusing magic rules

Ask ChatGPT:

- *"Polish this paragraph without changing the tone."*
- *"Does this scene contradict earlier events?"*
- *"How can I make this character's transformation clearer?"*

You'll be amazed what a clean pass can do.

Hour 15: Blurb + Title (9:00 PM – 10:00 PM)

Write your back cover blurb and title.

Prompt ChatGPT:

- *"Write a fantasy blurb for a story about a healer-turned-queen."*
- *"Suggest five fantasy titles based on this summary."*
- *"Give me a haunting final line for my back cover copy."*

Pick a title. Copy the blurb. Done.

Hour 16: Formatting and Saving (10:00 PM – 11:00 PM)

Turn your story into a shareable, readable file.

Ask ChatGPT:

- *"Help me format this for Kindle or PDF export."*
- *"What font and layout should I use for a clean, readable fantasy manuscript?"*

Use tools like:

- Google Docs or Word (for formatting)
- Canva or MidJourney (for a quick placeholder cover)
- Reedsy or Calibre (for EPUB/MOBI export)

Save final versions as .docx, .pdf, and .epub.

Hour 17: Sharing or Savouring (11:00 PM – 12:00 AM)

The final step: decide what you want to do with your story. You can:

- **Publish it** on Amazon, Draft2Digital, Wattpad, or your blog
- **Send it** to beta readers or friends
- **Keep it** for yourself as a complete work
- **Use it** as the seed for a bigger project

Ask ChatGPT:

- *"Write a short post to share my new fantasy story on social media."*
- *"What are five ways I can turn this story into a series?"*

You did it. One day. One world. One finished story.

This is your one-day writing ritual. You can follow it once, or a hundred times. With each pass, you get faster. Stronger. More focused. Your imagination sharpens. Your stories grow.

You don't need permission. You don't need to wait.

You have everything you need.

So open a new page, ask a wild question, and begin again.

The next fantasy is already waiting.

Doing It Again Tomorrow: Becoming a Fantasy Story Machine

You wrote a fantasy story in one day. You conjured a world, forged a hero, shaped conflict, bent magic, and saw it through to the end. That's no small feat—it's the kind of thing most writers spend months dreaming about. But here's the real magic: **you can do it again tomorrow**. And the next day. And the next. Not because you're superhuman, but because you now have the mindset, the tools, and the method to become a *fantasy story machine*.

This chapter is about shifting from one-off success to sustainable creative momentum. You don't have to write a fantasy story every single day (unless you want to!), but when you train your imagination like a muscle and give yourself permission to *write fast, write messy, and write with purpose*, you enter a rhythm that makes consistent creation possible. And fun.

Let's look at how to build that rhythm, stay creatively fresh, and become a writer who *always has another story ready to go*.

Build Your Daily Setup like a Ritual

Consistency thrives on **repetition**. To write fantasy stories every day—or as often as you want—you don't need to reinvent the wheel. Just show up and follow the process.

Each day, begin with:

- A fresh prompt
- A cup of whatever fuels you
- A 10-minute warm-up (idea generation, journaling, or reading a paragraph you love)
- Your story goal for the day (1,000 words, 1 finished scene, a full draft)

Ask ChatGPT:

- *"Give me a new fantasy story concept involving magic, betrayal, and a stolen crown."*
- *"Write a quick summary for a story set in a forest that moves on its own."*

These rituals put your brain in *writer mode* quickly and painlessly.

Create a Personal Story Template

To keep output consistent, build a reusable **fantasy story skeleton**—your personal structure. This could be a 7-chapter format, a three-act structure, or even just a list of beats you always hit.

Your base story might include:

1. Opening image of the world
2. Introduction to the protagonist's problem
3. Inciting magical event
4. A turning point or betrayal
5. Climax of internal and external conflict
6. Sacrifice or major decision

7. Poetic or thematic resolution

Ask: *"Create a one-day fantasy story beat sheet I can use every day."*

Now you've got a path to follow—every time.

Keep a Fantasy Idea Bank

The best way to stay productive is to never start from zero.

Ask ChatGPT to:

- *"Generate 20 fantasy story ideas involving forbidden magic."*
- *"Give me unique settings for fantasy stories—cities, forests, islands, skies."*
- *"List 10 character concepts for tragic heroes in a fantasy world."*

Save these in a doc or notebook. Next time you sit down to write, pick one and go.

Pro tip: Rotate themes. One day write a dark fantasy. The next, something whimsical or romantic. Keep yourself engaged by playing with tone and genre mashups.

Use Old Stories as Seeds for New Ones

That dragon you wrote yesterday? Maybe it has a twin. That enchanted ring? Maybe it shows up in another kingdom. You don't need to build a massive fantasy series all at once—but you *can* weave threads between stories and revisit ideas.

Ask: *"How could I turn yesterday's fantasy story into a connected tale in a larger world?"*

or

"What would a prequel or spinoff look like for this character?"

Now every day's writing builds something bigger—if you want it to.

Keep the Stakes Low, The Magic High

The point of writing fast and often is not perfection. It's momentum, practice, joy. You'll write some stories that feel clunky and others that feel golden. That's part of it.

Every time you write, you:

- Discover new corners of your imagination
- Get faster at making decisions
- Learn what kinds of stories *you* love telling
- Become more confident as a world-builder and storyteller

ChatGPT can help smooth the rough edges—but even if you keep a story raw, it still counts. You still made something from nothing. That's magic.

Create a Monthly Challenge

Want to level up? Set a 30-day goal:

- 15 complete stories
- 10 rough drafts
- A mini-anthology based on a shared theme
- A serialized epic told in short bursts

Ask: *"Help me create a 30-day fantasy writing challenge with daily prompts."*

You'll build endurance—and a fantasy portfolio in the process.

Reflect, Reread, Repeat

Every few days, look back at what you've written:

- Highlight moments or lines you love
- Note what surprised you
- Pick one story to revise or expand
- Write down a lesson you learned about storytelling or yourself

Ask ChatGPT: *"Help me write a journal entry reflecting on what I learned from today's story."*

The more you reflect, the faster you improve.

Celebrate the Identity Shift

If you've written a fantasy story in a day, you are already more than just a writer. You're a **story machine**. Not in a mechanical way, but in a magical, ever-flowing, world-conjuring way.

You now know:

- How to create from nothing
- How to use prompts to build deep, original work
- How to structure and finish fast
- How to write with emotion, energy, and vision
- How to repeat that process whenever you choose

So do it again. And again. And again.

Not because you have to.

Because you *can*.

And because the world inside you is too big for just one story.

You're a fantasy writer now. Not someday. Not when the book is polished. **Today**. And tomorrow. And the day after that.

You don't wait for inspiration. You meet it on the page.

And that's where the real magic lives.

I hope you found inspiration within these pages. If you liked this book, please leave a review where you bought it. Thank you from the author.

www.ingramcontent.com/pod-product-compliance
Lightning Source LLC
LaVergne TN
LVHW082341200926
848481LV00012B/3409
* 9 7 9 8 2 3 0 2 7 5 3 2 9 *